KEEPING IT UNDER WRAPS
BODIES, UNCENSORED

An Anthology

TRACY HOPE, ALNAAZE NATHOO,
LOUISE BRYANT

Editors

Keeping It Under Wraps

Copyright © 2023 Keeping It Under Wraps LLP.
All rights reserved.
71-75 Shelton Street, Covent Gardens,
London WC2H 9JQ

ISBN: 978-1-8384914-4-4

No part of this book may be reproduced or transmitted in any form, by any means, without prior permission in writing from Keeping It Under Wraps LLP.

www.keepingitunderwraps.com

To the reader who finds their story in these pages: we see you.

To the writers who shared their stories: thank you.

Table of Contents

Introduction 2

Dr Normallove: Or How I Learned to Stop Worrying
    Jessy Mijnssen 5

Gaze
    Heather Purlett 13

On Being a Real-Life Frankenstein
    Eirik Gumeny 23

Sin Lives Here
    Majini Ya Mombasa 37

Muscle Memory
    Julia Rudlaff 47

Paralysis and Passion
    KT Ryan 59

They Say It Is My Reptile Skin
    Adin K 67

Skin
    Beth Ann Jedziniak 73

'Stache
    Gabriella Brand 81

From Fins to Feet
    Sarah Lyn Eaton 91

Head, Shoulders, Knees and Toes, Knees and Toes
    Frauke Kasper 105

Staying in Touch
    Catherine Cronin 115

Doctor Face: A Facelift Story
    Kay Redrup 127

A Suit of Armour
  Natasha Cabot 137

Sex Ed: Mormon Edition
  Hillary Jarvis 143

Waiting for Weight Loss (and Other Things)
  Adrian Slonaker 153

Yours is Not the Only Erection in the Room
  Bruce Loeffler 163

The Little Lotus Flower That Could
  Aoife E. Osborne 183

My Journey to Full Exposure
  Iris Leona Marie Cross 193

Does Anything Taste as Good as Skinny Feels?
  Bex Thorp 203

Hairy Legs
  Premalatha Karupiah 211

Wardrobe Wednesdays
  Matt McGee 217

Social Justice is Key to Eating Disorder Recovery
  Sarah Wirth 229

How I Learned to Ask for Help in the Forests
  Nancy Rechtman 237

Dog
  Meredith Wadley 243

Afterword 252

Content warning: some of the essays in this book include topics such as suicide, self-harm, eating disorders, sexual abuse, medical and surgical descriptions, and other related themes.

The writers of these essays come from diverse cultural and generational backgrounds. Their voices and their views are their own.

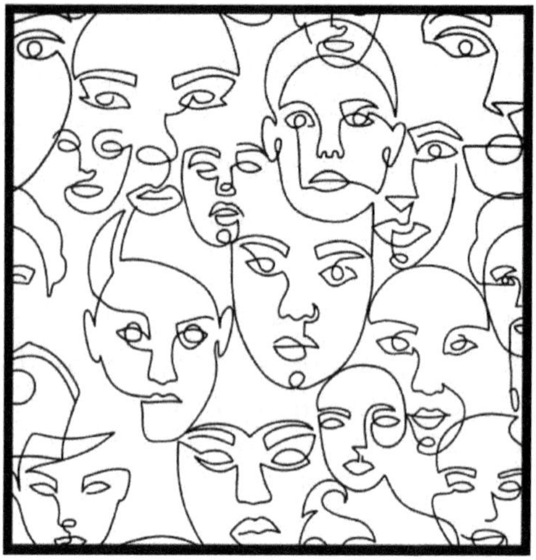

Introduction

Whatever the opinion, conversations about bodies are always polarising. There's the body positivity movement, those who state that the movement is irresponsible because it is normalising unhealthy habits, and then the general social media and celebrity culture that bombards us at every moment with unrealistic body expectations. From 'heroin chic' to Brazilian butt lifts, overly sculpted physiques to dad bods, filters and face tune, expectations are constantly changing and generally unattainable without surgery, untold hours at the gym and disordered eating moonlighting as nutrition plans.

We face difficult conversations when discussing disability, illness, pain, body changes and medical issues that are meant to be kept hidden due to the discomfort they cause others.

In many parts of the world, governments continue to regulate women's bodies and through that limit their very existence. And all of this isn't even considering cultural expectations - light versus dark skin, slim versus large hips, even tall versus short can have a traumatic impact on how we live our lives.

These discussions about bodies, while moving in the right direction, still have a long way to go. We need to embrace the normality of people being all shapes and sizes - the conversation should include disabled bodies, trans bodies, physiological relationships with our bodies, the negative impact the general cultural landscape has on bodies. We need to hear from people of all sizes, genders, sexualities, races, ages, and cultural backgrounds about how they live inside and present their bodies to the world.

The essays included in our third instalment of Keeping It Under Wraps aim to take control of this narrative, sharing real stories, from real people. From penis size to face lifts, dysmorphia to eating disorders, it's all there, nothing hidden. Our goal, as always, is to give our writers a chance to share their difficult stories in the hope that through these stories our readers will see themselves and feel less alone.

Dr Normallove: Or How I Learned to Stop Worrying

Jessy Mijnssen

Jessy Mijnssen

I got my first ostomy two months before my sixteenth birthday. I'd never even heard of one until the day before the emergency surgery to remove my colon. My first thought upon hearing the description of an ostomy was that I would never, ever have sex with anyone. I would be too disgusting. It was unclear at the time if my stoma would be reversible or not, but nine months later, it was reversed – to my detriment. Nineteen years later, I got a permanent stoma and at that point, I already had me a man.

By the time I had that first surgery, I'd been in hospital for three weeks to try to undo the nine months that I had spent hiding that something was terribly wrong with my guts. My very proper paediatric gastroenterologist, with his mid-Atlantic accent and his bowtie, had mentioned the possibility of an ostomy. 'It's a bit of intestine – just a few inches – outside of your abdomen that you'll wear a plastic bag around.'

I was horrified. He sent a stoma nurse to my room to explain what an ostomy would be like and answer any questions, but I didn't hear anything that she said and just kept explaining that I wasn't getting a stoma and that it was just a teeny tiny possibility. When she left my room, I was in a full sweat, though my apparent ulcerative colitis and the medications to treat it were often causing me to sweat, so it may have been unrelated.

As I was calling someone to rant at, the nurse came back in with a huge marker. 'I'm meant to mark you for your stoma,' she said.

Apparently, the doctor had just told her that my colon had gone toxic and I would be going into surgery shortly. The doctor later apologised for the order in which things had taken place, but I would indeed have that ostomy.

Throughout my sophomore year of high school, I felt like I was at war with my body. Once my colon had been removed, another flare-up of the disease revealed that I hadn't had colitis, but Crohn's disease instead, which can affect the entire digestive tract. For years, I would flare every spring and autumn. Eating, socialising, working, and getting an education all had to be tactically planned. Every morsel of food that I consumed had to be carefully considered for its effects on my body, my trips to the bathroom, night sweats, and so much pain and nausea. I had three sizes of clothes in my wardrobe: things that fit when I was flaring (often purchased in the children's section of the shop), things that fit when I was at my 'healthy weight' (a number assigned by Dr Bowtie that came from a chart's norms, according to my height) and things that fit when steroids had me storing water like some animal living in a desert. My eating was not only disordered by my fear of what food would do to me, but also by outsiders' positive reactions to my skeletal body when I was in an agonising flare.

After nineteen years of chronically flaring, trying new medicines that would eventually stop working, struggling with body issues, and cobbling together a life despite all those things, it was time for another big surgery. I'd already had near-annual surgeries for fistulas, which are little detours that the body makes around a sick bowel. They either connect to other organs, tissue, or the skin somewhere – my somewhere was always a labia. But now, it was time for a more aggressive cut.

My mother had recently died of colon cancer and, with constantly inflamed guts, my risk of developing cancer myself was sky high. I'd begun having some serious incontinence issues, which is not ideal for anyone, but certainly not for someone in their mid-30s. My healthy, handsome husband, whose body has never betrayed him, seemed willing to roll with whatever might come. We'd been able to maintain a loving, physically intimate (thanks to some creativity at times) relationship for ten years, and I'd warned him at the start that there was a big chance that I would one day require another ostomy bag. However, I think we'd both imagined that 'one day' would be around age sixty or seventy.

I'd naturally left the paediatric wing by then, and post-op, my buttoned-up older conservative surgeon embarrassingly told me, after having asked if I'd been able to resume the physical side with my husband, 'I never knew how you were able to do it previously.' Charming.

Still, he was the one who'd seen my constantly raw skin and expanding detours on a regular basis. He'd also been wary to give me a permanent ostomy because 'once we get in there, we don't know how much we may need to remove.' This could have meant not just the sick bowel, rectum and anus, but also the bladder, ureter, uterus, and fallopian tubes were at risk of removal.

For me, 'Your parts may be so sick and damaged that we may need to remove them' doesn't sound like a reason to keep my abdomen closed to leave that damage dormant. As luck would have it, only the parts they had intended to remove came out and the rest of my innards were remarkably well. I now had a 'Barbie butt,' which is what ostomates call it when your bum hole has been sewn shut. And I had never felt better. I loved my new stoma, and because she resembled the rosebud that Dr Bowtie had used to describe what a stoma looks like, I named her Rosie.

Two months after surgery, and after my eight weeks of recovery in which I had to be suuuuuper gentle with my body, I was on my way to a celebratory dinner when I saw my favourite statue in Zürich. Besides the familiarity of passing it regularly and the fondness that fostered, the reason that I love this statue is her figure. She is round-hipped and slightly round-bellied and proud-looking, with her hands on her hips and her posture upright. I'd once remarked to my husband how beautiful I found her to be, and he said, 'She's a bit fat.'

Preposterous! She has a silhouette very similar to mine and yet I thought that she was beautiful. I was both comforted and inspired by that.

When I was passing her that night on my way to dinner, filled with my slightly narcissistic love for her even though post-op weight loss had reduced the resemblance, I popped my spare (emergency) ostomy bag on her and took a photo. Wouldn't you know it? She still looked beautiful.

I posted the photo on Instagram with the caption, 'I've never successfully yarn-bombed anything, but I just ostomy-bombed my favourite statue in Zürich.'

I am lucky enough to live in a city rife with lovely nude statues and I was filled with a sudden desire to bomb them all. I'd gotten a box of two-piece bags post-op and discovered that they wouldn't stick on me, so I began using them to decorate the city. While my husband was away the next weekend, I took my dog and some spare bags and bombed some of my favourite nudes around the lake. Then I developed the habit of always having a spare bombing bag on me to stick on the ones that I happened upon in my daily travels.

After that, friends and family started texting me photos of statues that they wanted to see with a bag. At a visit to my stoma nurse, when she was lamenting how taboo ostomy bags still are in Switzerland, I let her know that 'someone' had been sticking ostomy bags on statues in town and she loved it. She gifted me a big box of pre-cut bags that had been returned and couldn't be used by anyone else.

I would take the backing off the bag and press the adhesive plate to my clothes a few times to make it linty so that removal wouldn't cause damage to the public art. I would look at these healthy-looking, classically beautiful stone bodies, with a plastic bag hanging from their hip and just adore how they looked. I would imagine young, pre-illness me seeing a bombed statue. I wondered what her reaction would have been then when she learned that she would be getting an ostomy.

Would she have thought back to that statue of David at Bürkliplatz and be comforted that her body would still be just as loveable and beautiful with a bag? I want future ostomates to know that they can have a normal love life and even love their own bodies, with or without a piece of intestine on the outside of their abdomens. And so, I bomb.

Gaze

Heather Purlett

Heather Purlett

When I was fourteen, I read a women's magazine. Then I took a fresh sheet of paper and wrote that I'd kill myself before I turned forty.

It was the nineties. Supermodels were celebrated and the fashion industry came under fire for upholding unrealistic beauty standards, so this particular magazine decided to run a feature about what a realistic body looked like and how it aged. They picked a white woman in her early twenties, five feet four, about a hundred and thirty pounds, had her dressed in beige underwear, asked her not to smile for the camera, and took pictures under an unforgiving neon light. Then they aged her, presumably with a combination of make-up, prostheses, and software. She grew fatter – except for when she started losing muscle – and saggier with age.

I was beginning to come to terms with the fact that my five foot two would never stretch to the coveted model's five foot ten, and that I was curvier than the gawky teenagers who wore designer clothes, cavorted under the sun, and looked good on the glossy pages. Hence my despair and decision to kill myself before my body and morale went too far south.

I was on holiday with my newly-divorced father at the time. He found the note and gave it to my mother, who came into my room one morning.

'You look beautiful,' I told her, because my father hadn't exactly complimented her physique in the years before they divorced. One of my main concerns at the time was to make her happy again. She didn't pay attention.

'Why did you say you'd kill yourself?'

There were embarrassed explanations because I'd forgotten about the note already and then a promise not to write things like that anymore. I went to school, got myself home, and before I made myself dinner, ate half a dozen chocolate bars and threw up.

When my mother noticed, she talked to me again about it.

'Don't do it. I used to do it, too, at a time when your father was making particularly cruel jokes about my size. I got an ulcer. So, don't do it.'

I nodded. I still did it.

***

The trouble with diet culture is there's a grain of truth: being overweight sets you up for health problems. The other trouble with diet culture is it makes you gain unnecessary weight and hate yourself in the process all while using the ridiculous fad diets and the diet plans over endless weeks that bore you to tears just reading them. There's a barely-exaggerated skit by Mitchell and Webb about lifestyle nutritionists. One tells the other to give the client an impossible meal plan, saying that either they keep it up and they die, and then they won't complain, or they give in and then it's their fault.

I'd always seen my mother on a diet. She considered her body too fat and too short, and a succession of low-fat food and powdery meal substitutes was supposed to help with that. She only stopped dieting in her early seventies when her heartburn got so bad she had to stop eating a lot of foods, including anything high fat. Then she became thin and she flaunted it. She flaunted it with glee while telling me not to become too fat – I was pregnant at the time and going through that one magical moment in a woman's life when she's allowed to gain weight. Arguments such as 'I'll put on the weight that is needed for my health and that of the baby' were not met with approval or even understanding. What mattered was that she was no longer one of the overweight ones.

My binge-eating fourteen-year-old self was terrified of putting on weight, but eating lots of sweets was the one thing filling her with warmth. I hated myself for, as I viewed it at the time, lacking the willpower to have anorexia like one of my relatives did. It started as a diet when she was seventeen, and everyone admired her weight loss. Even as her parents began to worry and her tricks to pretend she was eating even concerned me, it was hard not to see that suddenly, people thought she was beautiful and she'd become popular. She didn't know it yet, but her anorexia caused a hormonal imbalance that persisted long after her recovery. Eventually, her gynaecologist told her she was unable to have children.

In those troubled teen years, I had a tiny, wiry, scary woman as a gym teacher. One day, before a run, she gave the girls a speech. 'I know you get lots of pressure to be thin and go on a diet. But you don't need to worry about that and you don't need to pay attention to any of it. Eat well and exercise. That's all you need to concern yourselves with.'

She was right. I was afraid of her to the point of waking up early with a knot in my stomach on PE days, but I knew, deep down, she was right. Even as I gazed at models in magazines, binged on sweets and made myself throw up, I remembered her words. Respect your body, give it what it needs, and enjoy.

It's just that it was advice for reasonable people and not for me. I was convinced to the bone that I wasn't good enough.

***

In time, I weaned myself off binge eating by smoking (my teenage years were a peak time for healthy choices). When I turned seventeen, I started skipping certain meals just like my relative, sometimes for a whole day. I wasn't basing it on a certain diet; I just stopped eating. It felt so good to reclaim some 'willpower' for myself. The attention I got from men was the same, but my parents complimented my weight loss.

Years later, I bought a book about healthy eating habits. There was a questionnaire to fill. *What good things has dieting brought into your life?* Maybe the author was expecting readers to have their moment of realisation and write with tears in their eyes, *Nothing. Dieting has never brought me anything good, excuse me while I go and get some chocolate cake.* But instead, I wrote, *It's the only time my father spoke about me with pride.*

I searched my memory. He'd come to accept my choice of studies, and even acknowledged that my job was, in fact, a job that not anyone could do. But that didn't make him proud. No, it was dieting and being thin. The last time I went on a diet, I was behaving like the other women my age: watching myself and not eating too much, and I wasn't doing weird things like having my own mind even when it went against his. Even when I was getting my master's with honours, his eyes lit up with pride and affection only when he said, 'My daughter is on a diet' or 'You haven't gained weight'.

Two other young women I knew were dieting, too, because their boyfriends asked, or more to the point, demanded. They were both thin. One lived with her partner, who forced her to have only a meal substitute for breakfast – one of those sad protein shakes that tastes like ash. The other one was studying a more challenging and prestigious discipline than her man.

In stark contrast, the romance novels I read had one highlight. There was always a moment when the insecure heroine stood in front of a mirror while the hero told her to just take a look at herself, because she was beautiful, full stop.

Romance novels are that rare space where heroines are praised for enjoying their food while the men go to the gym and take care of their looks. I like to imagine the writer behind those heroes – she's middle-aged and her stomach is soft because she sits down a lot and likes to eat biscuits as she types fast to meet her deadline. She thinks about her readers; maybe she's met them. She thinks about those women and girls who break into a grin when they see her, the way they whisper, *Your books gave me so much joy when I was going through a tough time.* Or just, *I love what you do,* no need for anything else. How they each look unique and beautiful in their own way, even if it doesn't match the current standards. She creates heroines they'll identify with and gives them a hero that says, *Look at you. You're wonderful just the way you are.*

***

Heather Purlett

There's this old saying that to be happy, you should stop worrying about what others think of you, but we long for connection. We need approval – not from everyone because that's impossible – but at least from a few others. We need people we care about and who care about us. From our first moments until the end of our life, we need a loving gaze.

Maturity doesn't mean you stop caring about what others think. It means you choose whose opinion matters.

Going back to that piece that made me want to die before the age of forty, I wonder what the journalists even thought they were doing. Why couldn't they show that woman wearing flattering clothes? Why not ask her to at least look relaxed? Why not use a warmer, softer light?

I think it's because that's how they saw people outside the fashion world: ugly gnomes who need extensive shopping or maybe even surgery to look acceptable. Maybe it was how they saw themselves; maybe they had eating disorders of their own. They certainly didn't want to inspire suicidal thoughts. After all, you can't be dead and buy stuff, and their business relies on mildly to severely insecure recurring consumers.

The first ever models were shop assistants who looked somewhat like the wealthy clients they served. They were asked to wear the clothes so the clients wouldn't have to go through the hassle of undressing, but could still see what the apparel looked like on a figure like theirs. Why did models stop looking like most other people to become 'aspirational'? I stopped reading those magazines because I stopped seeing the point of staring at clothes modelled by girls whose bodies looked so different from mine.

Then came all the gossip blogs about the fashion industry and the cases about middle-aged men preying on

Heather Purlett

confused teenagers away from home, a.k.a. models ('It's what you need to do if you want to work in this industry'; 'No big deal'; 'Everyone else does it'; 'It's going to look bad if you say no').

One day around the same time, I caught a glance of myself in the mirror, and I didn't like what I saw – too short, too fat – so I decided to gaze at my body like the hero looks at the heroine in romance novels.

Now, thirteen years and two children later, I can't say I stare at my reflection with endless admiration – or that I have much time or desire to stare at myself anyway. I never aimed to look like the younger me again, even though my mother was perplexed when I told her I didn't want to go back to the figure of my twenties. My body tells my story: a mother with a bit too little sleep, active on her feet and fond of cake. And it's good enough.

On Being a Real-Life Frankenstein

Eirik Gumeny

The first thing I remember is Dr Kapoor's frowning visage staring at me from the foot of the hospital bed.

I had died, he explained.

Sometime between the surgery and this conversation, I had stopped breathing. *After* the hard part, he stressed.

Gruff and cranky on a good day, the doctor seemed more annoyed with me than usual, his arms crossed over his chest, his wild brows furrowed.

I had stopped breathing for several minutes, he said. Did I remember that? The gasping, the spasms, the panic and concern I had caused.

No, I answered.

The crotchety old Indian man continued to glare at me, weighing my reply. He stepped forward, putting his hands on the edge of the bed frame.

Did I do it on purpose?

No, I answered again. No, Dr Kapoor, I did not stop breathing hours after my double lung transplant on purpose.

***

Eirik Gumeny

Born with cystic fibrosis, I was told from a very young age that I'd be dead before I reached twenty. As years passed and I continued to be alive, however, adjustments were made to that prognosis, with the age of my untimely demise inching incrementally upward. That number, though, was always finite – and close at hand. Nurses and doctors, along with the occasional respiratory therapist, like coffin salespeople working on commission, seemed incapable of not reminding me that I was going to be dead far too soon.

Of course, once I was sick enough that 'soon' deteriorated into 'now,' once I finally bought in and started considering wood finishes and burial plots, the conversation shifted. *Transplant* became the new sales pitch. Death still loomed, but everyone was suddenly a lot more concerned with kicking the Grim Reaper in the balls than letting him have his way.

I was airlifted to a transplant centre a few states over and nursed back to *just enough* health to survive the operation, had a feeding tube attached to gain back *just enough* weight. I was given *just enough* drugs to keep from flipping the fuck out.

And then I waited.
For someone else to die before I did.
And then I flipped the fuck out.
And then I was given more drugs.
And then I waited.
For someone else to die before I did.

A compatible set of donor lungs can take anywhere from a day to several years to become available. There's simply no way to know with any more specificity. I was waiting for a healthy person – a young person, most likely – the same size, blood type, and tissue type as me, within a few hundred miles of the transplant hospital, to cease being a person.

There's no right way to do that, to hope and pray for someone else's family to give up on their hopes and prayers. The cold reality is that I was waiting for a heartrending tragedy to occur so that I might have a *chance* at a future. And as sick as I was – on oxygen 24/7, incapable of so much as brushing my teeth without assistance – I had nothing but time to dwell on that fact.

Unsurprisingly, I began to feel like a monster.

There are amazingly few moments in life when it's ok to root for someone else's death. I'd argue that awaiting a lung transplant *still* isn't one of those times. The odds of a serial killer, the exact same shape as me, dying non-violently and within driving distance were astronomically small.

And that was the best-case scenario. *That* was what I was watching stars for.

Otherwise, I'd have to face the fact that I was hoping for another person, another someone, tall and thin like me, but stronger, healthier, a someone with an actual *future*, to stop being all those things – to die, slowly, surrounded by their friends and family, in a torrent of sorrow and tears.

There is no way to reconcile that wish with still being a decent human being.

So you don't.

***

While the nursing teams were staffed by angels, the medical teams, especially the doctors higher up the food chain, had a tendency to see me as a name on a chart; a set of statistics; a *thing*. I was conflated with my symptoms, a medical condition that needed correcting and little else. Worse, I was a problem.

Doctors, of course, are very good at fixing problems. That is, arguably, all that they do. That advanced level of aptitude, however, requires an advanced level of confidence. Of arrogance. Of passion and belief in themselves.

In that way, doctors are a lot like NFL players. And, like those American football players, doctors don't always react well when things don't go their way.

I had been admitted to hospital a few months into my wait for haemoptysis – coughing up more blood than could comfortably be ignored or written off as a symptom of end-stage cystic fibrosis. I had been in and out several times during the two weeks prior, spitting up blood for an hour straight, then not again for days. Dr Ebrahim, another transplant specialist, couldn't figure out why it was happening and couldn't find where the bleeding originated. He had run tests and received only negative results. He had missed a vital update because an overnight physician hadn't felt like doing his job. Dr Ebrahim grew visibly aggravated, each day getting angrier and angrier at the problem.

At me.

After he had done all he could think of, with nothing to show for it, Dr Ebrahim stormed into my hospital room and blamed me for his failure to find an answer. I sat there impotently, near tears, with oxygen tubing and IV antibiotics draped across my scrawny chest, being accused of withholding the truth from the medical teams, purposely keeping them from stopping the bleeding inside of my failing lungs.

A few nights later, I began vomiting up blood relentlessly, ceaselessly. An emergency pulmonary embolization

– essentially, a cauterisation of the blood vessels in the lungs – was performed, saving my life. A minor miracle. The next morning, the entire transplant team poured through the room – doctors, nurses, administrators I hadn't seen in months, even some of the surgeons – marvelling at how not dead I was.

Dr Ebrahim came by that afternoon, laughing – *laughing* – at the unmitigated disaster the previous two weeks had been. He stayed and chatted for an astounding *five minutes*, possibly the longest uninterrupted stretch anyone has ever spent with a doctor. During that time, he admitted that he still didn't know what had actually caused the bleeding. He also admitted that not knowing something often made him upset.

That was the closest to an apology I've ever received from a medical professional.

***

Over time, I realised that no matter how the medical teams acted, no matter what they said, they were doing everything they could to help me survive and to give me my life back. Dr Ebrahim, like Dr Kapoor after him, accused me of sabotaging my own health because that was the only answer left to him. He had exhausted all other avenues. The angrier they were and the more they fought with me, the more they were fighting *for* me.

In the thick of things, though, with machines beeping and drugs coursing and death looming, it was hard to separate that understanding from the utter contempt radiating off them. Dehumanisation and a callousness toward suffering are built into the transplant process, though that's not something covered in any of the brochures. Detachment as a survival mechanism is something the patient has to learn on his own.

I spent the better part of a year in that existential limbo, slowly unravelling, vacillating between rage and depression, guilt and self-hate, rationalisation and fear, before I finally received The Call. Before I was cracked open and filled with a dead man's parts.

I spent three days in a drug-fuelled haze, upside down and underwater, struggling to right myself. When I finally broke through, I found myself attached to machines and strapped to a bed in a sterile ICU room, surrounded by strange doctors and nurses poking and prodding at me.

In short order, I was moved out of the ICU and into a step-down room, and then, as I continued to shed IVs and monitors, into a regular one – one with windows. The sun shone brightly as I was wheeled inside the room. Outside, flowers bloomed in an explosion of pastels; songbirds landed on the windowsill, chirping a tune just for me.

But the view wasn't the only benefit: now that I was on the other side of the transplant, everyone's attitude had changed. There were no more accusations, no more doubt. I had left the sepia-tinted Kansas for a riotously colourful Oz.

I almost felt like a real person again.

Almost.

During the surgery, I had been trussed up with chest tubes – plastic tubes, like thick straws, inserted through the skin and into the pleural cavity outside the lungs, draining the excess blood and fluid from the surgery into rectangular containers resting on the floor.

Five of these tubes jutted out of me as I began my rehabilitation, learning to breathe again, to walk again, wobbling around the hospital hallway like a newborn deer. As days blurred together and as medications changed, the chest tubes were the only constant – and the last hurdle that needed to be cleared.

Dr Johnson, one of the surgeons, came bounding into my room, chugging down a Diet Coke and almost literally buzzing. Without saying a word, the doctor injected a very slight numbing agent into my abdomen, then made small talk, completely reversing the generally accepted order of things.

Star Trek II: The Wrath of Khan was playing on the TV above my bed.

'You a Trekkie?' he asked.

I shook my head. 'Not really, not since I was a kid.'

'They're probably my favourite movie series,' he said, bright giddy eyes on the screen. 'I love them. I'm *in love* with them. I know them all by heart.'

And then, without warning, Dr Johnson shouted 'KHAAAAAN!' – completely in time with the movie – and ripped the first of the chest tubes from my body, very much the picture of a mad scientist. Drops of pleural fluid and tiny hunks of fatty tissue spattered across the bed sheets.

The nurse taped some gauze over the wound – the hole that went straight to my lung. No staples, no stitches, no glue. Then they did the same for the other chest tubes, only this time without the Shatnerian gusto.

And that was it. I was done with the inpatient portion of the transplant.

Before I could be discharged from hospital, however, I had to spend most of a day becoming better acquainted with the bucketful of prescriptions I would be taking home with me – a literal bucket, full of tablets and capsules and foul-smelling oral suspensions. A pharmacist had come into my room equipped with printouts on the order and timing of the medications. I was drilled like an army private, told to separate the medications into groups – antivirals, antibiotics, anti-rejection drugs – then told to do it again, this time by dosage schedule. I was lectured and quizzed. It was vitally important that I had all this memorised, that I could take my prescriptions in my sleep if needed.

I could.

With that, I was set loose on the outside world.

***

Acutely aware of the massive scar across my chest and the smaller ones dotting my abdomen, it didn't take long before my wife and I started making jokes equating me with Frankenstein's monster. My walking was awkward for weeks as the muscles in my legs were rebuilt. I was bloated and swollen for months, a wax figure of myself, a close approximation. Due to my severely compromised immune system, I had to wear a mask any time I went out into the world to keep from becoming contaminated with the germs and bacteria swirling around out there – to protect myself from the public, the huddled masses and wretched refuse and unvaccinated trust fund toddlers.

I went with a thick filtered neoprene half-face motocross mask, thinking it less obtrusive than the full-face, attached-cartridge, *Breaking Bad*-esque models. But people still stared and gawped as I lumbered past. Security guards pulled me to the side and radioed their bosses about what to do with me.

The stares, at the time, infuriated me. Strangers knew that something was different about me, that something was *wrong*. They fled from the sideshow freak wandering through the supermarket and pulled their children away.

Eirik Gumeny

I was supposed to finally be free of being a patient, a subject, a thing, but the rest of the world had yet to be informed.

With the clarity of hindsight, some of this may have been paranoia on my part, brought on as a side effect of one of the many, many prescriptions I was taking. The changing cocktail of drugs prescribed before, during, and after the transplant affected my mood dramatically. The high dose of prednisone, specifically, often made me irrationally angry. Others made me grumpy, sleepy, dopey – all seven of the dwarves. I was having trouble remembering things. I found myself thinking one thing and saying something else entirely.

I rattled off this laundry list of concerns at every opportunity. Nurses sympathised with my plight but offered no answers or assistance. Doctors, meanwhile, simply shrugged.

'Memory loss,' one explained, 'is one of the side effects of the drugs, and you need the drugs, so...'

The issue was dropped forever.

There was similarly no mention or acknowledgement of the horrific nightmares that still keep me from sleeping four years later. No warning about the survivor's guilt, or the PTSD, despite it being twice as likely for transplant patients as the general population, just a hair shy of soldiers returning from war. Divorce, as a former physician liked to remind me, is also incredibly common after an ordeal like this.

But that's always where the conversation stops. She had no advice, no further steps to *prevent* the divorce. The entire transplant process is about the physical aspects, about keeping the body whole and working. When mental health issues were brought up by the transplant team, it was only as those issues related to the patient's compliance. My doctor's fear wasn't that I might leave my wife; it was that if I did, I might get depressed,

I might get angry, I might get *too* messed up and stop doing what I'm told.

Now, to be fair, some doctors since then have been willing to admit that maybe, *just maybe*, psychiatric disorders appearing after transplant can negatively affect the patient in ways that don't directly affect compliance. But actually treating those disorders still isn't in their purview.

The *patient* needs to be the one to remain vigilant and identify and act on these issues, to reach out elsewhere if needed. The medical team can't be burdened with learning how to spot potential signs of a mental health issue – they're too busy making sure he's alive enough to have a mental health issue in the first place.

Over two years passed before I was able to identify which emotions were mine and which were prescribed. Over two years of raging and fretting, of feeling like a failure without a purpose, before I realised that I might have a problem and I might need help.

Over two years passed before I figured out who I actually was.

Dr Kapoor had never been one to mince his words or to couch himself in comforts. He said exactly what he meant, no more and no less. Presumably, this was part of what made him an excellent doctor – there were no miscommunications. I'm no longer his patient; I've been handed over to the post-transplant team. Dr Kapoor liked solving problems, and I'm not considered a problem anymore.

The last time I saw him was in passing, in the hallway of the hospital as I was leaving a routine check-up.

'You look good,' he said, sizing me up, admiring his handiwork before continuing on his way.

I *looked* good. A common enough phrase, but it felt telling of the whole experience. At the time, I was still pinballing between side effects, struggling with my very identity after shutting myself down for so long. But none of that mattered to Dr Kapoor because I *looked* good.

***

I'm not the only patient to have felt this way. In recent years, more studies have been conducted regarding the psychosocial stressors of receiving a lung transplant; textbooks are being written. Across the US, there are plans – and plans to make plans – for more comprehensive mental health treatments to be worked into the medical team's scope.

But, I wonder, will that be enough?

Will that keep future transplant patients from feeling left alone, abandoned by our makers and shunned by the public? Will that stop us from feeling like monsters, full of rage and doubt, strangers in our own bodies, cut up and put back together?

Probably not.

But if it can keep us from becoming lost in the darkness, it'll be a pretty good start.[1]

---

[1] *Names have been changed to protect the doctors' privacy.*

Eirik Gumeny

Sin Lives Here

Majini Ya Mombasa

Majini Ya Mombasa

Majini Ya Mombasa

'Malaya' is the word for 'slut' in my country. It's what men call women to shame them. The first man to call me 'malaya' was my father. I was around eight or nine years old.

Late one afternoon, I was trying on a pair of blue jeans I had borrowed from my friend when my father walked in. I had never worn any trousers before because my parents forbade it. They said trousers made girls and women look ungodly. When I saw Stella in her blue jeans, I wondered how God could not find my friend as beautiful as I did. He must have been blind. Stella was celebrating her birthday when she came to school in them and as we walked home after her party, I asked her if I could try them on. She promised to bring me a different pair the next day.

The following day, I wanted to get home earlier than usual to try on the trousers before my parents came home from

Majini Ya Mombasa

work. So, I made sure I did everything right. I completed my classwork faster than usual and submitted it to my class teacher. I neatly arranged my locker so that I wouldn't be told to do it all over again. And during PE, I finished all the exercises the instructor gave so that I would be allowed to leave the field earlier than the rest of my classmates. A few minutes later, Stella kept watch as I sneaked out of school.

When I got home, I took off my school uniform and took a quick shower. I thought the trousers were too beautiful to be worn on a sweaty body. I paired them with my best blouse, which I tucked in. I went into my parents' bedroom and took my first look in the mirror. There was something missing, something that did not make me look as beautiful as Stella. I took the hairband out of my hair, and as it slowly sprang into the glorious afro that it was, I was stunned. There it was!

I turned around and marvelled at my buttocks. They looked soft and moulded like dough in those jeans. I cupped them and shook them a little and giggled as they shook. Then, I turned around and whined[2] my waist.

I must have been lost in my own beauty because I did not hear my father come in. He stopped short when he saw me in their room. Then he charged towards me and smacked my face so hard that I fell on the floor. I felt dizzy as he grabbed me by my left arm and dragged me across the floor all the way to the sitting room. When we got there, he beat me with a huge cane cut from a neem tree.

---

[2] *Whining is a popular dancing style in Africa and the Caribbean. When you whine your waist, you move your waist in circles while keeping the rest of your body still. It looks like twirling a hula hoop.*

Majini Ya Mombasa

'Whose trousers are these?' he yelled repeatedly as my skin broke into tiny cuts from the lashes. I would not answer. 'Do you want to be a malaya?' he yelled. I said no even though I didn't know what 'malaya' meant. All I could get from my father's angry tone was that it was a bad word.

I don't remember how painful it felt as the lashes landed on my skin, because something else stuck with me from that day. I saw fear in my father's raging eyes and gulps going down his throat when he asked me that one question – if I wanted to be a malaya – over and over. I felt powerful. I had never seen my father terrified of a woman before. If anything, women, including my mother, were terrified of him.

From that day, I was intrigued by this mysterious woman called Malaya. Who was she? Where did she live? What did she look like? Was she as stunning as I was when I wore trousers? Did she also love blue jeans? Why was my father so terrified of his daughter becoming like her? Books were always my first place to look for answers, so I tried to see if there was anything written about her in the school library.

The second man that called me malaya was a strange man I met in the streets of Sikujua, a small quaint dusty village located in the heart of Voi town. It was a year after my incident with the blue jeans. I was walking home from school playing around with my chalk-pink checked uniform.

The previous day, I had watched the movie *Sarafina!* on a cassette that my dad brought home. I admired everything about Sarafina. She was smart, confident, brave, outspoken, and as beautiful as a cowrie shell. What I loved most about her was her school uniform. It looked just like mine, except that hers was black and short. I wanted mine to be that short.

Majini Ya Mombasa

I pulled up my uniform and folded it just a little bit above my waist so that it would be short. Then I pulled it a little bit higher until the hem was mid-thigh. I stood with my arms akimbo and sang:

> *Sarafinaaa in Soweto*
>
> *Na na na na na na*
>
> *Love you Sarafina*
>
> *Love you Sarafina*
>
> *Sarafina Sarafina Sarafina mama yo*

I sang at the top of my lungs and out of key. I walked as if the street and I had come to an understanding, as if the murram soil was more than willing to rise in support of my soles. With each stride, I started to feel like I was Sarafina at my core.

When the man stopped me to yell at me to pull down my uniform, I was so angry. How dare he cut short my reverie like that just when my soul was beginning to burn as bright as a firefly? I yelled back and made mocking faces at him. At that point, he warned me not to behave like a malaya. I quickly dropped my hands and fixed my uniform because I was curious whether this man knew who Malaya was.

'Sir,' I said, 'so you know this Malaya? I have been dying to meet her. Could you take me to her or show me where she lives?'

The man looked at me strangely and went on his way. As a kid, I used to wonder why that man left without telling me

Majini Ya Mombasa

anything about Malaya. Now, I break into bouts of laughter. Ignorance is bliss, aye?

The third man that called me malaya was my first boyfriend after he found out that I cheated on him with his best friend. In my defence, his best friend had gorgeous silky hair that curled like my pubic hair.

My first boyfriend wasn't the last. More men than I care to count have called me malaya. Some when angry, some out of enjoyment, and others when intimidated. As a woman, my bodily appearance and sexual awareness have both been unsafe, from the father who beat me about trousers to a bystander who watched me to an ex-boyfriend who thought it was his right to punish me for being promiscuous. I ferry a body around that I don't own. Instead, it has become this thing that men objectify and control, from what to wear to how to wear it and how it should and shouldn't be used.

I would be lying if I said the slut-shaming doesn't get to me once in a while. Like that one Sunday morning in 2012 when I lost my temper with the church youth leader for opening his calabash-shaped mouth to berate women for wearing bikinis and posting their photos on Facebook. I remember feeling annoyance slowly growing in my belly like a fire seed, and then flaming until I could no longer swallow it.

When he said, 'Which man do you think will marry you? No man wants to marry a woman who does not respect her body by dressing like a malaya,' I guffawed.

'Marry you? Pfft! Do you think any woman here dreams of being married to an ugly piece of walking shit? Your face is gaunt, hideous, and haggard with over-sized mismatched clothes over your jutting bones. This… thiiiis,' I said while pointing up and down to his appearance, 'is what you think women aim for?

Majini Ya Mombasa

What do you think makes you so special? That tiny pee pipe that you overcompensate for with your hatred towards women?'

He did what men who can't take back what they dish to women do. He charged at me, ready to hit me. 'How dare you talk to me like that?!'

I smiled scornfully as he frothed at the mouth.

I never went to church again.

Or that time I kept quiet as a man slung the word while we were out on a dinner date. I met him at a local conference and he had seemed pretty cool and nice. During our date, he sneaked in a 'polite' suggestion that we hook up seconds after giving a short speech laying claim to being a feminist.

I told him I wasn't interested in sleeping with him. He asked for an explanation and I told him I didn't have to justify myself.

'I don't understand why you wouldn't be interested. I have been a gentleman, took you out on a romantic dinner, paid for meals and drinks, and our Uber fare. What more must a man do for you to give it up?'

I did not respond.

He didn't stop there. He belittled my intelligence, called me unattractive and said that I should be grateful he gave me his time. 'Malaya wewe,' he said, ending his rant and waiting for me to respond.

I did not respond. I finished my meal, washed my hands, and left. I blocked his number on my way home.

Regardless of the times I have stood up to men like these, I am still subjected to insults and labels of whore or slut or bitch. I have tried to teach men, written numerous posts about it on social media, and have passionately spoken out against it in public spaces. But of course men, like God, could not be bothered by my concern.

Eventually, I made peace with the fact that to be a woman is to have a body that men want to control. No matter how I carry this body around, they think it is flawed. They call me boring when I am not sexually accessible to them but loose when I am. I am Malaya by virtue of being born a woman. I also learned to build my body to deal with the torrents of slut-shaming. I should not have had to, but I had no other choice.

This body of mine is unruly. It has refused to be beaten into covering itself as if it were a shameful thing. It has refused to be shamed as if it were a disposable sack of meat. It has refused to be decent to make men comfortable. It has refused to be godly for the sky daddy. This body wears blue jeans even in front of my father. This body wears short dresses and delightfully bounces on the streets as people stare in disbelief. Its warm thick thighs open in obedience to the lust this body has. Sin lives here. So God and men can go fuck themselves!

Muscle Memory

Julia Rudlaff

Julia Rudlaff

For a while, I was limitless. From age five to seven, I danced the way I was born to. I took every summer class that was offered, I practiced at home in the basement, and I begged my mom to let me stay at the studio until 9 p.m. so I could take classes with the older kids. Dancing fuelled me. It ricocheted me from being a kid to being a kid with a purpose. All I wanted to do was dance. I daydreamed about it at school, I showed up to the studio early and left late, and I choreographed my own solo when I was six. It was paradise. Sweaty, challenging, emotional paradise. I never wanted to leave. I never wanted to stop.

It was late, past 9 p.m. Everyone else had left the studio. My mom waited for all the other students to trickle out before stopping my jazz teacher at the door.

'How can we get Julia to lose her baby fat?' she asked.

'Cut out all fried foods, especially potato chips,' the teacher said without pause.

She walked away, carrying the class CD case and a tote bag. I listened intently from around the corner, feeling a new weight encircle my seven-year-old ribs.

Julia Rudlaff

Mr Alexei taught me my first variation when I was nine. It was the first ballet choreography I ever learned and I kept forgetting the word for it. Once I remembered, I would say it over and over and over in the mirror: *variation, variation, variation.* It felt a little magical rolling off my tongue, like it was infused with power and bravado and tulle. After that first lesson, I wanted to know every *variation* there ever was. I watched ballet performances on YouTube and practiced them in the living room. Once I tasted the adrenaline of flight and using dancing as a means for ascension into a higher realm, I couldn't get enough. I couldn't stop.

Mr Alexei told my mom that I could make it in ballet.

'She has the right feet and natural turnout. A good physique,' I think he said.

I left the studio feeling weightless, invigorated by a sense of purpose. *I'm gonna do it.* I was resolved. I was going to be a professional ballet dancer.

***

'If this is too much for you, too *hard***,** you should just go home and watch Saturday morning cartoons like the rest of the kids your age,' the ballet teacher in Chicago said. She was teaching a group of ten-year-olds intermediate ballet. She said the word *kids* with such disgust I knew I wasn't one of them. I couldn't be.

In sixth grade, I wanted to be a normal kid so bad I made up a whole narrative about who I was. I played soccer, enjoyed movies, spent my summers at camp and liked boys. But as soon as someone asked me what I liked to do, I told them. I shrank into who I was in fifth grade: the dancer; ballerina girl. I performed at the school talent show and my science teacher told me I should audition for *Dance Moms*. A lot of the other kids admired me or at least pretended to. Teachers were amazed by my dedication – my drive, as they called it. I was just disappointed I couldn't join the cross-country team because I had dance classes after school every day.

By seventh grade, I was just *the dancer.* One time, my advanced math teacher stopped me at his door before class. He reached out his hand and squeezed the stomach beneath my pink Abercrombie T-shirt. He said he just wanted to know what it *felt* like. He said he expected me to be skinnier, being the dancer and all. I went back to my algebra, but I couldn't find x. My build-a-bear body hadn't even been stitched together yet, but I already wanted to rip out all the stuffing.

I googled 'how to become anorexic.' A month later, my mother called me *anorexic brat* on a street corner in Chicago because I wouldn't eat anywhere that didn't have calorie labels on the menu and the nearest Panera was closed.

'You have such a good facility for ballet,' the ballet mistress in New York said. I smiled to myself, trying to be modest. *It's working,* I thought.

'We won't cast you as Clara if you don't gain weight,' the artistic director of my ballet school threatened, grabbing my bony elbow after class one day. 'No one will want to see a skeleton on stage.' I left the studio feeling numb and triumphant.

I was Clara in my first Nutcracker. It was advertised as the world premiere, with all new sets and choreography by a famous dancer from San Francisco. I was home schooling by then, so I had time for 1 p.m. rehearsals, 2 p.m. costume fittings, and 10 a.m. interviews with the local TV station. On opening night, when I took my bow in front of 2,500 people, my teacher, who was dancing the role of Drosselmeyer, told me I was going to remember this moment for the rest of my life. He was right. I

Julia Rudlaff

still have a Tupperware container full of fake snow from the snow scene. It's made from three-hole-punch scraps.

At a summer intensive audition for Charlotte Ballet (or maybe it was Pacific Northwest Ballet, or Houston Ballet, or Washington Ballet, I can't really remember), the auditioners had a form where they would rate each dancer on a scale of one to five in certain categories. The categories included: foot shape, arch flexibility, neck length, torso length, turnout, control, port de bras, turning, jumping, back flexibility, pointe work, and body proportions. This is why female dancers safety pin the number over the widest part of their hips – to make their bodies look narrower. To have the 'right body proportions.' The audition fee was ninety dollars.

I almost quit at the beginning of my first year in the full-time professional training division. I was dancing nine hours a day, five or six days per week, working out at the gym, and doing intermittent fasting to stay 'in shape.' I wrote a list in my notebook of reasons to stay and reasons to leave. After I was cast to perform a corps de ballet role in the professional company's *Peter Pan* shows, I was so elated I crossed off the entire 'reasons to quit' column.

My roommate had a breakdown one Tuesday after rehearsal. She was eighteen and I had just turned seventeen. That day, the teacher threw a CD at her for not knowing the barre combination. We were living together in a one-bedroom apartment in Cincinnati. Her family was in Texas, mine in Michigan. We were there because we couldn't let go of our nine-year-old dreams, and neither could our parents. We hated ballet but couldn't escape it. She said it felt like an addiction. That night, when she was sobbing on the floor, between her proclamations that she should throw up everything she eats or kill herself, I asked what she would do if she quit. She said she would dance on Broadway. I said I would to go to college. We both said we'd eat more.

We both showed up to rehearsal the next day.

The goal in ballet is to make it look effortless. The teachers used to say, *make it look easy; never let the audience see your pain.*

I had a panic attack onstage while we were performing a run of *Aladdin* for groups of schoolchildren. While I was getting ready, I noticed the costume was too tight around my chest and would barely clasp. I had to carefully distribute my breath within my ribcage so the ends of the bra would meet. I remember swallowing tears in the dressing room, embarrassed that these eighth graders would see my cleavage. The costume was so tight it constricted my breathing. I'm not sure if this prevented a meltdown or hastened it. All I remember was the sensation of tears carving a path down my foundation as I smiled and smiled and smiled for the kids.

I finally quit over pinkie fingers. The ballet mistress critiqued the angle of a corps de ballet member's pinkie finger during a *Sleeping Beauty* rehearsal and I stood in the back of the studio, appalled by the absurdity of it all. I laughed all night after rehearsal, finally seeing the ridiculous standards I had been holding myself to since I was nine.

'Passion' comes from a Latin word that means 'to suffer'. I wrote a poem once about how much I loved ballet. That love was not always a lie. Everything I did for ballet I did because I loved it. The weight loss, the bleeding feet, the hip scraping, the workouts, the perseverance through pain. I could've given up, but I never wanted to. Maybe it was Stockholm Syndrome; maybe it was passion.

During tech week before the professional training division showcase, the ballet mistress asked what I was going to do after. I told her I was going to college. She looked at me with pity and said, 'Don't worry, I know a dancer who went to college for four years and then got a contract with the Pacific Northwest Ballet. Anything's possible. You can always come back.'

I left the studio feeling mournful. Elated, but mournful. Coming down from the high of dancing again felt like free falling off a rock-climbing wall, with the life I could have lived catching me at the bottom.

***

I quit ballet at seventeen and didn't step foot in a studio for almost four years. I couldn't. It would be too familiar. Too inciting. I feared it would send me spiralling. I thought about taking classes for fun, and maybe even joining the contemporary company on campus, but I never did. *It wouldn't be good for me,* I told myself.

After I quit, I wanted nothing to do with ballet, dancing, or the arts in general. I couldn't stand any of it. Ballet broke something vital in me – some spirit I once had was choked by the toxic fumes of perfectionism, body standards, and relentless competition. I had to leave. I had to get out.

I did. I dragged myself out piece by piece until I was nothing but a ghost in the studios. Gone on to college, to a new life. For three and a half years, I lived as if it never happened. Except for the nightmares, relapsing, and panic attacks, I moved on. A part of me started fresh, while a part of me was still haunted, but all of me wanted to leave it behind.

'My body just wasn't built for this,' I used to tell myself after failing again and again to mould my body into a ballet body. I had the legs, feet, neck, and face, but my shoulders were too broad, my hips too wide, my breasts too pronounced.

Since I started taking ballet seriously at nine, I lived under the illusion that I couldn't possibly live a full life and dance. If I was a dancer, I couldn't cut my hair, I couldn't eat ice cream, I couldn't go to summer camp, and I couldn't stay up late because not getting enough sleep can mess with your metabolism and cause weight gain. I had to wear dangly earrings to make my neck longer. I had to study ballet videos on YouTube. I couldn't see my friends.

No, I always said, I can't go with you to the movie. I have to stretch. No, I can't go tomorrow either, I have to stretch. Every night: I have to stretch and work out. After nine hours of classes and rehearsals, cross training is essential. I have to work out and I have to practice. I don't have time to hang out with you, I have to practice. I have to sew a new pair of pointe shoes. I have to sew a new pair of shoes and I have to break them in before Monday, so no, no I can't go with you. I need good shoes for this rehearsal, don't you know it's very important? Don't you understand? First impressions are everything. Some of us don't have the luxury of looking the way you do so we have to *work*. Some of us weren't born to be ballerinas. Some of us have to *try*. Besides, I don't even want to go with you. What you want is a life and what I want is ballet. Can't you see we're different? I'm above you like that. I *want* to be here, doing this, working, working, working, proving myself. Demonstrating my dedication for no one to see but me. In the mirror, I'm not crying, just sweating in the gym in my apartment complex in Cincinnati where I live, as a sixteen-year-old, not wishing or daydreaming about homecoming or homework or senior year.

Julia Rudlaff

No, I never think about those normal things. They don't even cross my mind anymore. Not even when my high school friends come to visit, not even then, not ever. I don't think about it. College? I don't even remember what that means anymore. It's too dangerous to even consider. All I can think about is this body and ballet; this body that needs to be different so it can fit into the costume that the costume shop has from twenty years ago. No, I don't want them to alter it for me. No, thank you, I'll alter myself instead. Do the elliptical until my boobs magically go somewhere else. Until my shoulders retract. Until my body stitches itself into a different shape. The costume will fit. It'll fit, it'll fit, it'll fit, I promise, just give me a few more weeks. Just a few more, I'll be ready by tech week, I swear. I can do it. By tech week, I promise.

I lived in solitary confinement with myself and the stories I told, always trapped under the narrative that I could do anything if I just pushed myself to the brink every single day. If I just resigned myself to a life of studios and workout videos and kale. If I sacrificed loudly and cried quietly. If I agreed to want for nothing but applause at the end of the performance. If I just did those things, I could do it.

I looked at the girls who could do both with such envy. The girls who went to class and the club. The girls who got first cast and ate ice cream after dinner. The girls who had friends. The girls who didn't plan to stop eating two hours before class and three hours before performances. The girls whose bodies never needed to starve to fit into the costumes. The girls who could dance *and* live.

Why can't I be like them? I used to wallow. I could never find the balance. I could never walk out of the studio and leave my teachers' voices at the door. I had to be all in all the time and I just couldn't sustain it. My body couldn't sustain it. My mind couldn't sustain it.

Now, I show up to class as myself. I dance as myself. I do not shave or wear clothes that don't fit or put my hair into a bun with one hundred pins. The simplicity brings me to my knees. I am full of gratitude and remorse. I wish I'd known earlier. I wish I'd known I could've walked into a studio with a mullet and unshaved legs and not been scorned at the door. I wish I'd known I could eat four slices of pizza before class and not be laughed at because the teacher could 'see my lunch.' I wish I'd known I could go to a party and a dance class in the same week. My life never had to be so divided. I could be me and a dancer. A writer and a dancer. A geologist and a dancer. Queer and a dancer. A friend and a dancer.

The voice that used to scream *you don't belong, you don't belong, you don't belong,* was beginning to whisper: *there's room for you here. All of you.*

Paralysis and Passion

KT Ryan

KT Ryan

I didn't know whether I'd ever be able to kiss again. Not the peck on the cheek kind, but the passionate and DNA-sharing kind. That deep-throated kissing where tongues dance and mouths seal tight enough to breathe in each other's heat. Since my surgery, it seemed unlikely. Facial palsy had paralysed half of my face. Even the most careful sips of water sent liquid dribbling down my chin.

I shouldn't have been wondering about kissing. I'd just had a brain tumour cut out of my head and a jagged row of staples lined my skull. My forty-five-year-old body had taken a beating from the surgery in other ways, too. I was permanently deaf in my right ear, and it would take weeks to regain my balance. Those disabilities seemed more manageable, though, once I'd experienced the horror of a mirror. Staring back at me was a woman I no longer recognised – half of my face drooped like a bulldog.

Skin hung over my eye and pooled off my jaw as if one side of my face had melted. My blue eyes, which once fluttered with long lashes, no longer worked in unison; one of them couldn't blink or close, remaining wide open until a nurse finally hid it under a pirate patch. My neurosurgeon explained what I'd already figured out: I could feel my skin, but eating, drinking, and speaking were all challenges. He didn't mention kissing, but my mind drifted to my last kiss with my husband not long before the surgery.

I don't know what my husband thought about my face. Or kissing. I didn't have time to find out. Four weeks and six days after my surgery, he asked me for a divorce. I know he didn't leave me *because* of my facial palsy. We'd had problems for years. Still, I'll never forget how, during an argument with him earlier that day, my spit had gathered in the corner of my palsied mouth and splattered across his broad chest. I'd tried to hide my reddening cheeks under a veil of my blonde hair, but it didn't matter. I was leaking vulnerability all over the place.

After the whiplash of surgery and divorce, and once my three children had settled into their new normal, friends suggested that I wade into the dating pool. By then, I could at least drink a martini without it spilling from my lips. The right side of my face could move ever-so-slightly, but it was still a lazy and disabled companion compared to its left counterpart. If I tried to smile, the resulting effect was a freakish smirk. *What did these date-pushing friends not understand?*

First, there was the issue of what photo to upload to dating sites. Would I use a pre-palsy photo with my old symmetrical smile? Whatever fish clicked on my profile and bit would end up feeling duped once they saw my face. The other option was full transparency, which meant offering my palsied face up to a camera. My stomach churned at that thought, and so I never followed through in joining a dating app. What would I have written in my profile anyway? *Heads up, this fish can't kiss!* I couldn't even pucker my lips to blow out my forty-seventh birthday candles, never mind lock lips with a man.

KT Ryan

The first passionate kiss I'd ever seen was in the original Parent Trap movie. God knows my British mother and Irish father hadn't exchanged saliva in front of me. I remember watching the movie as a child, my bum nestled deep in the comfort of my mother's handstitched beanbags. My understanding of intimacy changed the moment Maureen O'Hara and Brian Keith finally gave in to their characters' mounting sexual tension. He cupped his hand around the flesh of her exposed neck and pulled their lips into such a fierce exchange that it sent a bolt of life into my pelvis.

I didn't expect to feel that bolt of life again after my surgery and divorce. I had built back my inner confidence and was thriving as a strong and independent mother, athlete, and writer. I'd even figured out how to appreciate my reflection again. However, I'd been using my facial palsy to shove my sexual desires aside.

Then I met someone.

I hadn't really noticed him at first, but he was one of the many regulars on the pickleball courts. I'd taken up the sport but was more interested in releasing my post-divorce rage on bright green plastic balls than noticing who I was playing against. As the months passed and I became more comfortable in my abilities, I found myself drawn to his hearty laugh, killer serve, and lettuce hair that curled out from under his Oakland A's ballcap. I began talking with him between matches, always from under the cover of my visor and sunglasses. He didn't need to know that one of my eyes still couldn't blink. When he made me laugh – which he did every time we talked – my hand instinctively covered the right side of my mouth.

A few months later, he invited me to hit balls with him at night. It sounded like a date. I texted back 'yes' before I considered my problem. The bright lights over the courts would illuminate my facial palsy. I could no longer hide under sunhats and reflective shades. I walked onto the courts slowly that night, running my fingers across the cold metal fence before turning to face him. Before we'd even picked up our pickleball paddles, he'd said something funny. I responded with a cockeyed grin, which made me look more smug than entertained. I knew I couldn't restrain my smile forever. I just wanted to marinate in the illusion that he might not have noticed the constraints of my face.

We continued meeting alone, late at night, playing between the blue and white lines on the court. Him on one side of the net, me on the other. I wondered how long this could go on, how I could preserve the physical distance between us so that he couldn't get too close.

'Want to go get coffee?' he texted me one Saturday morning. I chewed on my thumbnail, furious that he'd broken our spell and worried that we'd lose the magic of our easy banter once he sat close to me. He'd be able to stare right at my face where he'd have a clear view of its uncontrolled contortions.

Across a café table from him, my hand shook as I brought my latte to my mouth. Whether I could sip without dribbling was entirely dependent on the width of the mug's rim. I focused my eyes on his and swallowed while he talked. *Sip, swallow, sip, swallow.* The idea of what could come later between us – if there was a later – hummed between my legs while terrorising my mind.

Later that night, after hours of nonstop conversation, we laid down on my bumpy jute rug, absorbing the ethereal melodies of Cigarettes After Sex. His hand was inching closer to mine. My heartbeat jumped into my throat. We hadn't discussed *it* yet. The limitations. What my lips couldn't do.

It hadn't occurred to me to consider what my lips *could* do.

He rolled on his side to face me, his mouth inches from mine. The syrupy smell of caramel popcorn floated on his breath, and I inhaled it deep inside of me. I had to say something, didn't I? We had to talk about my facial palsy. Acknowledge it. Process it. And yet there he was, his full lower lip glistening and ready.

I propped my head up on my elbow to re-establish space. I wondered if he noticed the heavy effect of my facial palsy, how gravity pulled millimetres of skin towards the carpet. Was he staring at my eye? Before I could answer my own question, he reached up and held my cheek in his palm. I inhaled sharply and drew back. He removed his hand, apologetic. There, left on my skin was the mark of his cold, clammy sweat. He was nervous too. Emboldened by the touch of his sweaty palms, I grasped the ends of his fingers and pulled them back to my face.

Then we were kissing. Little ones at first, as if we were middle schoolers trying to find our way. My mouth couldn't drive the kiss but that didn't stop his from exploring mine. Soon, I relaxed into his touch and my lips began feasting on the silky smooth skin of his. Every nerve ending was awake and hungry for more contact. I let my body take over my mind and gained confidence. I recruited my tongue to skirt the ridges of his teeth and slid my wet finger across his lips. He pressed against my mouth for more.

I can't pretend that every touch went smoothly that night or the nights that followed. We had plenty of times when my teeth hit his, or I'd feel that little bit of saliva leaking out the side of my semi-cooperative lips. But I knew something now that I didn't know before. My body – my lips – could kiss again. Better than I could have ever imagined.

And with a hell of a lot of passion, too.

They Say It Is My Reptile Skin

Adin K

Adin K

When I was about eight years old, my world turned upside down. My mother's expectations of me turning into the most beautiful girl with a pretty smile and shiny hair withered. My entire body had turned red, and my hair had to go. I had developed a strange kind of itch on my body, but because I was a child, I would gladly forget about the itch the moment I had something else on my mind – longing to go back where I came from or asking for a penny or two the moment I heard the *falooda* vendor in the street. As night approached, my mother would scratch my scalp with a comb and remove all the flakiness from my hair. It became my mother's routine task because I had developed acute psoriasis.

It started with a red spot on my cheek, and before I noticed anything unusual, it flared up and spread throughout my whole body. That was when I was eight, but I was never an absent-minded or carefree child. I always carried an existential quest within me, sometimes sitting for hours in one spot to contemplate something. My father's absence for two whole years had affected me much more than anyone expected.

We were living in a valley where my family and I were supposed to spend two years with our extended family and

Adin K

without my father. It was the most beautiful yet frightening place, but I made friends, including with the girl no one else would sit with in class. She had more important things to say than the other children.

She was given to her parents in a plastic sheet when she was born because she had severe ichthyosis vulgaris, commonly called fish scale disease. I never sensed a hint of resentment in her words towards herself even though the rest of the kids tried. I sat with her throughout my two years there. Although my condition was hidden, I felt closer to her than anyone else. I also didn't relate to anyone else in that disturbing school with no rules against bullying or physical violence. I was unaware of these feelings back then, but now, after two decades, I can make sense of what happened.

Psoriasis, in one way, is the manifestation of one's mental state. It erupts during severe mental distress or depression and spreads under stress. My psoriasis is a reminder of my mental health. It tells me immediately if I am going through something. It told me the first time it erupted, and it keeps telling me throughout my journey. At least, this is how I make peace with it now.

Making peace with my body is a challenging task. Some days, I wake up in the middle of the night with my whole body itching and burning; other days, they are there, but they are resting silently on my body without creating any disturbance. Some days, I have to apply black liner gels to my hairline to hide the flakes; other days, my hairline is clear like it's never been any other way. During extreme summers, the sweat rolls over the scars and it burns as if someone has thrown salt on my exposed wounds.

Adin K

There are days when I can't wear anything white because my scars bleed, so I prefer to wear darker shades. Pastels are my favourite, but I can only wear them when I am not under any stress. I spend almost every night layering up my skin with steroids to smooth the dryness away. If I do not, I bleed and leave traces of my skin everywhere. It's a lifetime struggle and sometimes I cry out of pain, anger, and vulnerability.

My mother tells me it's a secret and a weakness I am not supposed to share with anyone. I followed her words my whole life, but one day, I broke the rule. And to my surprise, sharing it freed me – of the burden, the shame, the anxiety over being caught.

Mothers are primarily right, but when it comes to my body, only I can make the best choices.

Now I wear my scars with a little more comfort. It is me. This is how I am. When I own them, my body still itches, but a little less. It bleeds, but I look at my body with sympathy rather than hatred. It helps. Getting psoriasis was not my choice, but how I live with them is under my control. It is up to me if I want to live with hatred for my body or to recognise the condition as a part of myself and make peace with it. I choose not to make my pain worse than it already is.

Now, I go around and I meet different people. I do not apply gel liner to my scars anymore. When someone mentions them, I tell them about it. It is still hard with the burning, the bleeding, and the itching, but being open about it relieves some of the pain and boosts my confidence. In turn, such freedom helps reduce my stress and anxiety, which further lessens my flare-ups.

Adin K

    To all my fellow psoriasis fighters out there, body positivity is nothing but releasing the shame, which makes up more than half of the weight of this condition. You have been carrying more burdens than your chronic condition and you don't have to anymore.

Skin

Beth Ann Jedziniak

Beth Ann Jedziniak

Wearing skin is tricky. Owning pillows of flesh is difficult; I don't mean the difficulty of movement. That is easier to manoeuvre than the damage done by unkindness. That is the heavy stuff we carry around.

My friend Matt is a bodybuilder and has won awards for his muscle mass. When we went out to dinner, the waitstaff would look from him to me. You could see it in their eyes. They were trying to figure us out. What was a bodybuilder like him doing with someone like me? Twice we were asked how we knew each other. I looked down at my shoes. He looked the waitstaff in the eyes and said, 'We're friends, friends hanging out and having dinner.'

My friend Brian's wife was upset about Brian and I taking long lunches together until she saw me. Not met me. Saw me. Then she didn't care how often Brian and I had lunch together.

One day at work, one of my co-workers looked out the window as a client walked across the parking lot and said, 'Oh my god, that woman is *huge!*' I knew that my co-worker looked at me through a lens of love and didn't see me the same way, even though the stranger and I were similar in size. I asked,

'How would you feel if you overheard someone commenting about my size?' She got quiet then. Silence can be golden.

Wearing skin is tricky. Owning pillows of flesh is difficult. And by difficult, I mean that some people aren't careful with their words.

Most of the insults hurled now are an inside job. It's me repeating all the hatred spoken over my body. It's me taking the side of abusers who are long since dead. It's me saying yes to shame. I don't always say yes to shame. But sometimes I do.

The other day, Shame came calling and stomped through the house wearing heavy boots. I yelled, 'You little fucker, we don't allow shoes in the house!' He slipped off his boots, tiptoed over, and tapped me on the shoulder. For a few hours, I sat with him as he soaked me in shame, reminding me that even my own father couldn't love me.

Wearing skin is tricky. Shame sometimes hides in the folds of flesh.

As an adult, I felt that my dad's hugs were the perfect barometer of my weight, his hugs more accurate than a scale. When my weight was down, he held on and whispered, 'You look good. You look like your mother,' which was confusing because he left her too. He left all of us – here one day, gone the next. Off to live with another family. When my weight was up, he quickly tapped out of the hug, saying, 'You've gained weight.' My shoulders would round then, and my ribs would surround what was left of my heart, and I would whisper, 'I know, Dad.' I felt like I owed him an apology for weighing more but being less.

In high school, I grew steadily in stature. No one would penetrate this armour.

Beth Ann Jedziniak

Wearing skin is tricky. It makes us visible. It makes us unseen.

By the time I was twelve years old, strange men gawked at me as I walked by, thinking that I was older than my years.

The summer before seventh grade, a man stopped his car, looked me up and down, and tried to pick me up. I told him no thank you. I knew what that look in his eyes meant; I had fallen victim to it before the blood began to flow. He drove by me five more times. Slowing down. Gawking. Licking his lips. The next year, I ran into him in the hallway at school. He was the resource teacher. By then I had gained weight and lost my curves behind mounds of flesh, so I knew I was safe.

When I was eleven years old, I lived in a cabin in the woods of New Hampshire with my paternal grandmother and uncle. There was plenty of food, but that, along with love and affection, were doled out sparingly. The only loving words spoken were the ones my uncle spoke over me as he performed unloving acts.

It was in that cabin I began stealing and hoarding food. All the good food belonged to my grandmother, and we were instructed never to touch it. The only sugar consumed was stolen and eaten in secret. I knew I couldn't count on the adults to take care of me. I wasn't falling for that one again.

Shortly before I turned eleven, I was 5'6" and weighed 116 lbs. I know this because the school nurse weighed me and yelled my weight across the room for the secretary to write down, and all the kids gasped. I wanted to die then. I had the body of a young woman – breasts, hips, blood. But I was still a girl.

My grandmother bought me my first bra for my tenth birthday. She forced me to hold the bra and matching panties against my body as my uncle looked on, hungry for more than birthday cake and ice cream. I cringed, dropped my head, rounded my back, and tucked my breasts safely between my shoulders, making a cave. I wanted to crawl into myself because the outside world was unsafe. What should have been a rite of passage, receiving my first bra, was just another cruel joke and I was the punchline.

My dad left when I was nine. He had been slowly disappearing like a photograph left in the sun, disappearing by degrees, until poof, he was gone. When my mom had her next nervous breakdown, we were sent to foster homes, and then my little brother and I went to live with our grandmother and uncle in a cabin in New Hampshire with no running water.

Wearing skin is tricky. It breaks so easily.

Then Jesus took bread, broke it, and said, 'This is my body, which is given for you. Do this in remembrance of me.'

When we were still an intact family, each time my mother was committed to hospital, I would find a peanut butter and jelly sandwich made with Wonder Bread on the kitchen table when I got home from school. I didn't have to wonder where Mom was – the sandwich told the story.

When I was ten years old, my uncle took my body in new ways, broke it, and said, 'Your dad would hate you if he ever found out.' And I believed him. My body broken for my uncle's pleasure. I watched as my body obeyed his commands and then listened as my mind testified against me.

When I was seven years old, the age of reason, I went to confession for the first (and only) time in my life, and I lied.

Forgive me, Father, for I have sinned.

I lied that day because the truth was too horrible to confess.

Beth Ann Jedziniak

I lied because I had been told to never tell.

I prayed to God, begged him to save me. But he proved impotent. Or at the very least, uncaring. I lied that day because I already knew that no amount of Our Father's or Hail Mary's, no reciting of the Act of Contrition, would have any bearing on the state of my soul – a soul that I knew had been darkened to the point of no return.

The day after my non-confession, I wore white, walked down the aisle with my hands clasped in prayer, and the priest put the body of Christ on my tongue. He tasted bittersweet.

I was a normal-sized kid until foster care. In the cabin, my body turned on me, became other. And I turned on it when I became free of that place. I would not trust that body ever again. Even as a normal-sized kid, I wasn't safe. I'm not sure why I thought size mattered and would save me.

I was taught long before I was at school that my body was not my own. When I was older, I made sure no one would want it, including me.

Wearing skin is so goddam tricky.

'Stache

Gabriella Brand

Gabriella Brand

There are two kinds of girl moustaches: the funny kind and the sad kind. I've had both. The funny moustaches are made out of milk or ice cream. I sported them above my upper lip at various happy times throughout my childhood, like when I was down at the Dairy Queen with my friends, our bicycles thrown to the ground and each of us holding icy vanilla milkshakes in tall, waxy containers. We'd laugh because school was over and the summer was long and ice cream moustaches were inherently humorous.

The other kind of moustache wasn't funny at all. Mine first appeared sometime towards the middle of Grade Six. It was the harbinger of puberty and boxes of Modess.

A boy in my class pointed it out.

'Freak show, freak show!' He thrust his finger at my upper lip and sneered.

I must have looked confused.

Gabriella Brand

'You've got a moustache like the Bearded Lady,' he explained.

I'm sure I blushed, but with my olive complexion, a gift of my Italian ancestors, perhaps the blush wasn't so obvious.

A few other boys gathered around.

'Gabi's got a moustache, Gabi's got a moustache!' they started to chant.

By then, I wasn't holding back the tears.

We were on the field for recess. Miss Pedersen, our teacher, was standing just a few steps away from us. Blonde and blue-eyed, Miss Pedersen's skin was as pale and delicate as a Scandinavian winter sky. She was not the sort to have any kind of moustache, ice cream or otherwise.

She came over and put her arm around me. She was young, with a gentle way about her.

'It's ok, Gabi,' she whispered.

The teasing boys had run off by then, but she shouted for them to come back. She insisted that they apologise.

I was grateful to her, even as I could feel hot embarrassment moving into my belly. I hoped I wouldn't throw up. I sucked in my sobs.

We formed a little circle: Miss Pedersen and I plus the guilty boys. But soon other kids stopped playing games and jockeyed for a place near us so they could hear too.

No doubt Miss Pedersen thought she was being helpful by giving a thorough explanation of feminine facial hair. She went on to talk about Grade Six girls growing up. Then she mentioned different ethnicities and how people of Italian descent often have dark hair. (There weren't a lot of Italo-Americans in my posh Waspy suburban school). She talked about the fact that dark hair is often visible on the upper lip. It was normal *for those kinds of people.*

'I'll bet even Gina Lollobrigida might have some hair on her face,' she said brightly.

This was in the late 1950s and the sexy Italian movie star was a household name.

I wanted to die.

That night, I looked at myself carefully in the bathroom mirror. The boys were right. I was a freak.

Bristly black hairs were growing like fungus over my upper lip. If I turned in either direction, the moustache looked smudged, the way my math paper looked if I erased an answer over and over. I tried pulling the wiry hairs out with my fingers, but I couldn't get a grip on them.

There was no question about it: I would never go to school again. I'd have to stay in my room with the covers over my head. Perhaps the hairs would grow so long that I'd have a handlebar moustache like Buffalo Bill.

Mother cajoled me out of bed the next morning, assuring me that I could find products which would take away my unwanted hair.

'Forever?' I asked.

'No, just for a short time. Hair grows back.'

She tried to tell me that I was nowhere near Freak Show status, but I didn't trust her judgement. She didn't have a moustache herself. My dark hair and eyes and skin had come from Papa. Mother had light brown eyes and auburn hair. Her complexion was fair. What did she know about grooming olive-skinned girls who looked like Groucho Marx and who were dead ringers for the Bearded Lady?

Gabriella Brand

That afternoon I got on my bike and pedalled into town. All the hair removal products on the shelf at Power's Pharmacy seemed alike. There was *Nair* and *Neet* and a few others. I picked one in a pink box. The model on the box looked serene, with a face as smooth as a porcelain sink. Her bare arms held a bouquet of pink roses strategically across her chest like a naked Miss America.

I pedalled home and rushed into the bathroom. I stripped off all my clothes and took a quick look in the mirror. I was an ape. A veritable ape. There was no question about it.

Without reading all the directions on the bottle, I took a wad of cotton balls and dabbed the cream liberally on my upper lip, down my sideburns, around my neck, and up and down my arms and legs. I even found one or two hairs on my toes and dotted them with the white goop, although I left my newly-sprouted wisps of pubic hair alone.

Soon the stringent odour of ammonia filled the bathroom. I sat down on the covered toilet seat and waited. I was feeling light-headed. The swans on the wallpaper seemed to flutter, float, and drift off before my eyes. The mosaic floor grew wavy. Finally, I realised that I should probably open a window for some fresh air while I waited for the product to do its job.

Soon my entire skin began to itch and burn as if every hair follicle were on fire. Did the stinging mean that the product was working really well?

I waited some more, breathing hard, my eyes watering.

Finally, I wiped off the cream and saw little black hairs on the washcloth, scythed down by the toxic lotion. I looked at my forearms. They were the colour of strawberries, but there was no hair. I examined my thighs. No hair. And my upper lip, while swollen, was as bald as a baby's bottom.

I threw on a bathrobe and ran downstairs to show my mother.

'Oh, you did this yourself?' she asked. 'I was going to help you choose a product.'

I thought she would be proud of me. But she looked slightly alarmed.

'You look awfully red, honey. I think you're having an allergic reaction.'

She pulled me over to a window so she could get a better look.

By now my skin had erupted in thick scarlet patches, wrinkled and peeling like a boiled tomato.

She quickly made some cool compresses and covered me from head to toe. My upper lip looked bulbous and raw.

Mother asked me how much hair remover I had used.

'The entire bottle,' I answered.

The swelling eventually went down and within a few weeks, my little moustache grew back. Mother suggested I pluck it with tweezers, but keeping my errant hairs under control was like keeping dandelions from taking over the front yard. I'd pluck one and six others would grow in its place.

In high school, I submitted to electrolysis. The brusque technician who first treated me assured me that I was not, by any means, her worst case.

'You have just a dusting,' she said.

Then she proceeded to zap each hair with a little needle that made a buzzing sound like one of those anti-mosquito machines.

Gabriella Brand

'This procedure will permanently remove your hair,' she assured me.

It didn't.

After university, I turned to waxing. I'd go to a fancy salon and the aesthetician would lead me to a private room away from the other clients. She'd paint my upper lip with hot wax and then rip off the hairs with a sticky strip like a bandage on a scraped knee. I'd look clean-shaven for a short time, like a young recruit, but then I'd have to return to the battlefield.

As I grew older, I got used to taming my 'stache. After a pregnancy or two, it became a mere shadow of its former self and I rejoiced. But then, with age, the lip hairs returned slowly and steadily, like mould taking over the bathroom shower.

I'm still doing battle with unwanted hair, even at my advanced age. I tell myself it's silly. I talk to myself about objectification, male standards, feminism. And so on and so forth. But I can still hear those Grade Six boys calling me Freak Show and I know that hairs on a women's upper lip remains a subject of mockery and derision. If I thumb through a women's clothing catalogue, I might find androgynous-looking models, obese or big-boned models, mannequins with disabilities, and beautiful people of all ethnicities and races, but I won't find many women with facial hair.

Most of the dark-haired women I know find themselves running on the endless hamster wheel of moustache removal.

These days, I'm into threading. I discovered the practice during a trip to India. Back home, I put myself into the hands of Deeba from Karachi, who has her own threading salon here in Connecticut, and an easy-going acceptance of hairy upper lips. All her daughters have moustaches too, or they would have, if

Deeba herself didn't stand over them with her slippery thread and coax those hairs to surrender.

I like going to Deeba. Her place is lively and comfortable, with chatty friends and customers coming and going, and plump pillows on the couch. When I go there, I feel as if I am no longer alone with my dark pelage. I'm part of an international community of dark-haired women on whom moustaches grow naturally, the way aubergines or mint grows in a garden. There are Pakistani women, Middle Eastern women, Turkish women, Latinas, African Americans and others.

I enjoy lying back in Deeba's comfy chair under the bright light and puffing out my upper lip with my tongue. This creates the stretched surface necessary for the spinning thread to catch the smallest of hairs.

Deeba mows down my moustache with a few brief strokes, like a landscaper with a Weed Whacker. It's all over in two minutes and I thank her. I give her a little bit of money and she puts her arms around my shoulders and blesses me.

'Go in peace and return,' she says, and I do.

From Fins to Feet

Sarah Lyn Eaton

Sarah Lyn Eaton

Everything changed all at once – which is how it usually happens. People who don't use Tarot think that the Death card is the worst card to get, but I shudder when the Tower crosses my path. It represents extreme upheaval. Though not necessarily an ending, it does mean a dismantling of everything you know first.

All at once.

***

I didn't know what had happened. It was so strange. I didn't know where I was or why I was there. There was just gauze and the sound of oxygen pushing into me and beeping machines. I knew I was in a hospital, but I didn't seem to be able to stay conscious. I couldn't feel my body.

I figured it was bad. I let myself stay under, just in the shadows of my mind. Later I would find out that I had been in a coma, and that I was in the small percentage of people who retain coma memories. It's not what you think. It's not like I was aware of what was happening in the room – that would have been too easy. I did not know what had happened and I was aware that something was happening to my body, but my brain tried to translate those sensations into stories.

There was a lot of horrific torture. All the torture I endured in that coma world was based on the very real and deep debridement that was being done to me. And it wasn't real. And it was.

I had been on fire.

I did not know how bad the burns were. There was no feeling from my breasts down, though I could wiggle my toes when I was asked to. I didn't understand why they kept asking me to do that, but they said I was doing it.

I couldn't feel myself doing it.

I had almost lost my legs right away. I had severe third and fourth degree burns on my body from my waist to my ankles. My legs were covered in two-inch-thick burn gauze. I could see them. I could touch them with my bandaged hands. But I couldn't *feel* them. It was like this void space.

The hospital was hoping the skin grafts would take and that I wouldn't lose my legs. They were confident I would keep them, though, and fairly certain I would walk again. But there were still many more surgeries to go and anything could change.

Anything could change. At any minute. I had already learned that.

The dressing changes in between surgeries were painful. And necessary. And painful. I know that muscle is not meant to feel the air blowing across without its skin covering. The Burn ICU staff was amazingly patient and kind and tender when they could be, and firm and steel when they had to be, even when my belief that I could get through those trials wavered.

I kept my legs, minus some muscle tissue. As a kid, I was a tap dancer. I even got paid to tap for a couple of summers of Summer Stock. In hospital, trapped in my hospital bed, I dreamt of tapping again after I was discharged and after I had more surgeries. More debriding. More painful dressing changes.

I was dreaming of tapping again because I still couldn't feel my legs. I was a singer, dreaming of auditioning again and putting myself out there. I was ready to start living.

I regained more feeling in my torso, where they had taken skin from donor sites where I had not been burned, to graft onto my legs. I trusted them that some feeling would return. I was very confused as to how I could not have any feeling in my legs while they claimed I would still be able to use them.

Muscle memory, they said. But what about the muscles that burned away? What memories did that muscle hold? What of that memory had I maybe lost? What if I couldn't walk?

They started to shift me from a bed to a chair and I felt like a torso supported by cement pillars. It was terrifying. I could feel that I was standing on the floor. I could feel the floor beneath me. There was resistance beneath my feet. But I couldn't *feel* the floor.

How could that be if the nerves in my feet were undamaged?

It was hard for me to hold on in my very drugged state of trying to stand without falling over. My nerves had burned away. All of them. In both of my legs. Everything. I wondered if they would come back, but the staff couldn't tell me. They hoped they would and said they should, but they could not guarantee anything.

I had so many questions, laying there in my bed, tracing the track of the privacy curtain as it cut its way through the ceiling tiles, following it over and over again. I tried to brace myself for an uncertain future. Would I face a life of checking my legs for cuts and bruises that I couldn't feel? Could I master walking without having sensation?

Could I share this body with a void?

***

My days were full of encouraging voices and visits from my wife and family and friends. I could believe then that everything was going to be ok. At night, the shadows and fears danced at the corners of my room. The Other World I had spent my coma days and nights in slid overtop the reality of hospital.

Sometimes I had my legs, but I couldn't walk. Sometimes they were amputated. Each world had its own terrifying moments of not being able to save myself, of being strapped to a bed, unable to escape, or sitting in a chair I couldn't get up from. I'd ask for help only to find, over and over, there was no help for me.

I thought my heart would break through my ribs out of terror. I dragged my body through a broken window, the glass cutting into my arms, as I tried to get away from the wolves. I can still feel it all.

Then I would wake in this world and this reality. My head was underwater, my heart was drowning, but I was still breathing. I was so razor-focused on learning to walk, there were still things I hadn't realised. Like, my voice was so soft almost no one could hear me. I couldn't sing.

I had been so terrified in the coma, not knowing what was happening or why it was happening, that I had fought the intubation tube. With every exhalation, I pushed it up and out of my throat until they taped it down around my mouth, but the damage I wrought had already been done.

***

Sarah Lyn Eaton

When I left the ICU, I was able to walk to the end of the short hallway and back to my bed. Then I needed a nap. Every step was a huge trust exercise, and my walker was a necessary crutch. Without the nerves to transmit electric signals to my legs, the working synapses had to find a new way to get their demands across.

I had to relearn how to walk and climb stairs. In the gymnasium, a large room full of equipment and physical therapists working with patients, there was a set of stairs. It was three steps up to a platform and back down and it was daunting.

I couldn't lift my foot up more than one-quarter inch off the ground. I really believed stairs were impossible, but my PT was amazing. She would lift my leg up and put my foot on the first step. That was such a strain, but I pushed gently into it. We would chant over and over, 'Up, up, up, up…' Then we would lower my foot back to the floor and chant, 'Down, down, down, down…'

We did this for days, over and over. I couldn't do it without help. I didn't think I ever would. I was getting frustrated, thinking that we were wasting my time on a futile exercise.

Until one day, we started chanting 'up' and my foot twitched in response all on its own! I still wasn't able to lift my foot, but you would have thought I had reached an impossible mountaintop.

That was the moment I understood that we were reprogramming the electrical synapses in my nervous system, the ones that had burned away. My brain was learning to find other pathways to get messages to my feet.

It was working.

My coma nightmares followed me to the rehab unit. The nurses there all asked me what had happened, but I didn't know what to tell them. I wasn't sure what was real or what was coma real. And talking was difficult. It was also work. Just like moving my legs.

When my PT asked me how the connection to my legs felt, I had to think about it for a while. After all, I hadn't been thinking, I had just been doing. I was frustrated because I had been having trouble with pain in my feet, even though my legs were blank voids. My feet hadn't been burned. So, what was wrong?

I ruminated on it at night, stuck in my bed, and an image impressed itself upon me. If my torso was the mainland, then my legs were the superhighway that led to my feet, the solitary islands. Imagine the islanders woke up in the morning to discover the highway had vanished. If I were one of them, I'd be burning shit down trying to get the mainland's attention.

Or I would drown in the ocean, trying to reach the shore again.

That helped me. I started to talk to my feet like they had their own sovereignty. I apologised to them for the accident. I asked them to work with me, to help me rebuild those pathways. I asked my feet to be patient.

***

I doubled down and did everything my PT asked of me. I had low days – a lot of them. I was a fall risk and I spent time unable to get out of my chair without the presence of a nurse. When I was allowed some independence, I wasn't allowed to leave my room, but soon I was walking the hallways with my walker, and eventually, a cane.

I liked to walk.

Sarah Lyn Eaton

Walking required, and often still does seven years later, utter mindfulness. I have to think about how the muscular system works together and try to remember which muscle has to move first when I lift my leg. Then I have to see where my foot goes and move the right muscles to put it back down gently onto uneven ground.

Only then could I answer a question or finish telling a story. It was a slow process. Snails and sloths were faster than me.

But I was moving. I was in motion.

I was so slow that the world felt like this undertow waiting to catch a hold of my shuffling steps and drag me under. The world moves so fast; so much faster than it needs to. I did not know how I could ever match pace with it again. My legs couldn't run if they had to. If the undertow gripped me, my weak body would never be able to swim out of it. My legs would never protect me. They would never outrun a tsunami. They would be my hindrance.

Walking felt like stilt walking. My legs were thick columns, almost hydraulic, holding me up and doing as I commanded. But they weren't *my* legs. They were on me and they were part of me, but they weren't mine anymore.

I didn't know who they were.

I was so sluggish, timing how long it took me to walk the twelve steps to the bathroom, that at night I imagined oceans and flippers and swimming without the need of walking. I could feel myself flying through the water. Sometimes, I just floated along the bottom of the ocean, all dark and quiet and easy motion.

***

One morning, as my wife was tending to my dressing changes, she brushed a spot on my leg and I cried out. It felt like I had been shocked. She thought she had hurt me, but it was the opposite. I had *felt* her touch while I wasn't looking. Mostly my legs were still kind of numb and felt like they were swaddled in cotton gauze, but I was overwhelmed with this sudden sensation of *everything*.

That spot began to grow and more spots of feeling bloomed. I'm one of the lucky ones. Not everyone regains full sensation, let alone so much sensation. Even though I could remember, to my newly grafted skin, everything was happening for the first time.

Have you ever seen a child running around bare-legged as toddlers, and as a wind picks up, they stop, squealing in both terror and delight? Like they aren't sure what they're experiencing? I have had the great pleasure, as an adult, of experiencing goosebumps for the first time. There was this weird moment when my brain said, *I remember goosebumps*! But my brand new skin responded, *oh my gods what the hell is attacking me!*

This was the moment I understood and made the connection that my skin, even though it was harvested from the rest of my body, was reborn and new. It was growing, acclimating to the new soil it was laid upon. I started talking to my legs differently, reassuringly. I coddled them. When they were cranky, I commiserated with them. Some days I let them skip a dose of lotion.

We never laid in bed, though. I had had enough days in a row trapped on my back where I couldn't walk. As long as they were able to move, we were getting up.

***

Sarah Lyn Eaton

They told me it would take a while for the nerves to grow back, but I missed the part where they told me the nerves in both legs would grow back at the same time. It was a trial. It was horrific. It was necessary. I still cling to that, desperately. It was a necessary step in healing, but for months, there was only more pain.

It was so bad that I often questioned the lengths the hospital went to in order to save my legs. I was angry. How could pain that bad not make one feel fire on the inside?

I didn't understand how the little mermaid could give up her voice for legs when she had a perfectly splendid tail. My singing had always been the way I emoted. Even when I kept my voice to myself, I had shared it with the woods and the mountains. It was how I pushed unwanted emotions through and out of my body. And I woke up with a whisper of words and a throat that can't play the notes anymore.

As the nerves grew back, every step I took was painful. I would have to stop and cry twice on the way to the bathroom. It was months of sinking into a depression because I had trouble holding onto the idea of having pain-free days on the other end of the regrowth. I understood what the mermaid had encountered on land: I, too, was walking on glass with every step.

I walked over shards of glass for months and learned how to be quiet in a world that moved too fast to hear my halted thoughts.

In the original tale, the mermaid returned to the ocean. I fervently hoped things would get better, because I could never return to who I was before. I was stuck with these legs and feet.

***

After the nerves finished regenerating, I noticed sensation start to creep back into my legs. I could finally feel when I was brushing against something, but I couldn't discern whether it was my cat or the coffee table.

That was strange, but it was progress.

Due to the burns, I have trouble regulating my body temperature. I suddenly found that I did not understand the language my legs were using to communicate with me. They just shouted at me.

Wah! If I didn't have a blanket covering my legs, I assumed I was cold.

Wah! If I had a blanket on, I would assume I was hot.

I was trying to dance on glass and I wasn't very graceful. I was a fish out of water, but there was a promise that I could learn the steps. My legs and I, we would figure it out.

And we did. We still are.

I had multiple outpatient surgeries to remove more scar tissue to increase my mobility. I did rounds of outpatient physical therapy and speech therapy. My legs started to talk.

Then it was like new roommates had moved in – there were two limbs on my body with varying and independent needs. The healing progressed at different rates, which makes sense since there was different damage to each leg. The left leg was burned deeper and had lost muscle tissue. It is definitely the more difficult of the two.

They don't always get along. Sometimes one wants to walk when the other wants to be elevated. One of them almost always hurts and it's frustrating. We exist as three roommates constantly scrambling to cover the rent. Sometimes, some of us have to do more work than the others, which requires more negotiation and mindfulness.

Still, they walk and talk and every day we understand each other better. They are capable of surprising feats when they are called to action, even if it requires extra care on the other side.

There is seldom a happy ending in the original fairy tales. Which is ok, because this isn't a fairy tale. This is my story. My days have pain and discomfort, and I am still slow, but I am not trapped in a tower.

We're figuring it out one step at a time.

Head, Shoulders, Knees and Toes, Knees and Toes

Frauke Kasper

Frauke Kasper

'Head, shoulders, knees and toes, knees and toes. Head, shoulders, knees and toes, knees and toes…'

I lie in bed desperately seeking sleep, but my mind is busy singing along on repeat – this song that I hated as a child and still abhor. But it's stuck in my head and it gets me thinking about all the body parts missing in the children's song that's supposed to teach us about our bodies.

One crucial body part I've been thinking about a lot? The womb: my first home and the place I originally come from. Not a picture book birth but a rather traumatic emergency C-section. Born blue, my blood was flooded with my mother's adrenaline. Her fear transferred to me through the umbilical cord that had nourished me for over thirty weeks.

The womb: a central part of my body, and my own personal source of creative power and a carrier bag for storing stories – mine and my lineage – for storing hurts, and for carrying around the past as well as the future.

The lungs: that filigree organ that keeps me going. Air in and air out. When I breathe, I do so much more than inhale and exhale. I ground myself. I calm myself. I absorb a multitude of information: something is burning; I wonder what that perfume is called; the cake will be ready soon; you, my son, need a shower; there's a thunderstorm coming.

As I toss and turn, anxious to sleep so that I won't be too tired tomorrow, my mind repeats once more.

'Head, shoulders, knees and toes, knees and toes…'

***

What I learned very early about my body:

The head is incredibly important. 'Put that helmet on or you're not skiing today!' My father's words are harsh. My mother is trying to gentle them by explaining, 'It's where your brain lives. The thing that makes you unique. Something that can't be fixed if broken, that can't be mended with a bandage or an operation.' It always seemed ironic to me that my father, having protected our heads religiously throughout our childhoods, would have a brain bleed when I was only just on the cusp of becoming a teenager. His body was never again able to fully follow his brain's instructions.

Shoulders are the perfect place to carry the weight of the world. In the mind of six-year-old me, it seemed perfectly rational to assume I could fix everything and everyone. I piled on everyone's problems, thinking that if I only tried harder, worked harder, or managed to catch the change in moods earlier, everyone's pain would disappear. With every failure to save my tiny corner of the world, those shoulders hardened a bit more.

Knees are the best indicator of the correct length of a school uniform skirt. Weaving social norms into my being, telling me what is allowed and what is not. Instilling the fear of seeming inappropriate, of showing too much leg.

Frauke Kasper

Toes are allowed to be tickled too hard, making me squirm, hating every second of the fabricated fun.

The song is still playing on a loop for only me to hear. 'Head, shoulders, knees and toes, knees and toes…'

***

What I learned later about my body:

My head is often home to thoughts of worry. Brain cells connected to nerves, sending signals into my limbs, into my bloodstream to beware, be careful, be liked. My analytical powers wasted on imagining every last thing that could possibly (or impossibly) go wrong. My creativity wasted on painting detailed worst case scenarios.

My shoulders curled over my babies while breastfeeding, keeping the world out a little longer. My shoulders curved forward to protect my overly sensitive heart. My shoulders tensed from too much typing, too much sitting. Initiating a rounding of the back that made me smaller, seem more insignificant, signalling to the world: please don't let me or my body be seen.

My knees shaking whenever I need to speak in front of a group of people and present something. These knobbly collections of cartilage that absorb the shocks of jumping, that bend with every step I take.

My toes desperately craving attention. They get stuffed into socks and shoes Cinderella-style so often that they have forgotten their natural shape, spending most of the year hidden away. Underneath the layers, they love bright colours and want to be pampered.

***

Frauke Kasper

And more, so much more:
My waist is perfectly shaped to hoist up a baby, a toddler, and nowadays a laundry basket. There's a movement, a shucking of the hips that settles the thing to be carried exactly right – although the long-term effects of straightening one leg while the other bends to push out the supporting hip and create that perfect ledge were completely unbeknownst to me until I needed to see a physiotherapist.

My womb, asleep for such a long time, but then waking, waking. Slowly calling in all that she would need for me to hear her. I had booked a Kundalini yoga retreat for March 2019 in the UK with a friend. I paid the deposit and asked my mother-in-law if she would be willing to stay at our home and help with the kids. But for some reason, I didn't book the flights. I still can't explain what stopped me or why but I simply didn't. Then as the date came closer, there was an email saying that they were unsure whether they could host the retreat: too few sign-ups, people were unsure about Brexit, they hadn't decided but they would probably have to cancel. A small sigh of relief escaped my lungs.

A day or two later I found something else entirely: a website offering a womb wisdom immersion in Portugal. The text spoke to me on an elemental level. I wanted so much to go there, even as it scared me, even as a deeper part of me knew that this would change everything.

I'd had three babies, a miscarriage, was married, and was an adult woman but had no real connection to my womb, my pelvic floor or my innermost core. It's fascinating that we study Venn diagrams, photosynthesis, the passé composé, Greek tragedies and the economy but we are not given an inkling of the power we carry inside us, of the creativity that lives within us, of the vastness that is our womb space. We are told to hush and be quiet and be good.

I booked the womb wisdom immersion even though I couldn't even get myself to tell my husband where I was headed. Instead, I told everyone I had booked an alternative yoga retreat (not completely wrong but also not the whole story). I booked without a discovery call, without having spoken to the woman holding this space, without having attended any of her other offerings or courses. I followed and trusted something that was flowing through my blood (a pulsing, a knowing): my intuition, which I now know resides in that deepest part of myself, sitting on a velvet throne inside my womb cave.

My intuition does not shout. She knows that I'll get there eventually. She speaks quietly but with conviction and I've learned to heed her advice.

There are other parts of me that live there: the lost child craving attention, and above all, love; the wild woman that has ancient wisdom to share; the mother that nurtures, nourishes and builds a home but has a tendency to martyrdom and wanting to control things; the student eager for learning, for development, for growth; a queen sovereign, able to guide from behind; a girl skipping along in a rainbow-coloured glittery skirt wanting to eat popsicles all day long.

'Head, shoulders, knees and toes, knees and toes…'

There is a freedom we carry inside our bodies as children before we are told about the big bad world where we must not show skin, before we have concepts of what is considered beautiful, before we learn what movement should look like.

Frauke Kasper

On my retreat in Portugal, I was given space to move, to scream, to squirm, to shake. I was asked to move past the barriers of shame, of the group, and most importantly my personal beliefs about myself. The question that crossed my mind the most often was: can I do this?

Shamanic breath work is a special breathing technique that takes you on a spiritual journey. I spent one and a half hours dancing with my eyes closed. In yin yoga, we held each pose for fifteen minutes – it was excruciating, even though the basic poses you hold are stretches lying down. By staying in a spinal twist for that long, tiny parts of muscles I had never noticed before started pulsing. Releasing stories held inside the body through movement was a new concept for me and I became comfortable analysing, talking, and thinking about all of this. It was novel to move through the pain, settle into my feelings, and allow my body to speak.

At lunch on the second day, we were asked to remain silent for twenty-four hours, just as the first bonds between us were building. We were talking loudly, gesturing wildly, and starting to feel comfortable with each other. We don't realise how often we use our voice until we are asked to remain silent.

On the fourth day, we worked through another barrier. After a deep journey, dropping into the somatic on an elemental level, I found the screams that were trapped inside my throat. So often I swallowed the pain, I put on the brave face, and I would endure the discomfort, but my body suddenly found a release – vocal, primal, incredibly physical – echoing through my entire being.

When I later connected to my womb space, I found that there was a lot more here than the ability to grow my children. There was a void, but now it felt like potential and opportunity and possibility. Not a black hole to fear falling into but a warm embrace, a welcoming back. Physically burrowing down into child's pose, toes pointed and curled under my legs, knees opened, shoulders relaxed and softening towards the ground, head bowed and resting on the yoga mat, I was invited into a new season of creation.

After an afternoon of movement and journaling, sharing things that I had buried and that would leave me with a vulnerability hangover, I walked down to the small stream where ice-cold water gurgled past me. My toes submerged first, then my knees. Lowering myself softly, my breath grew flatter – it was surprisingly hard to continue breathing normally when I was surrounded by the cold water. There was an urge to hyperventilate. Physically, my body does not like the water anymore. Something happened at some point – the waves of the Pacific tossing my body and throwing it onto the sand only to lift it back up and spin it around like I was stuck in a washing machine.

My lungs began to burn as fear pumped through me. I often physically shrink away from water, yet on that afternoon in Portugal, after screaming and sinking fully into myself, my whole body and my whole being submerged itself in the stream. Shoulders and head included, all of me was washed in that ice-cold water. It felt like a cleansing, like a baptism, like a rebirth.

My womb had been a black box for such a long time. Simply ignored. Not discussed. Not consciously a part of me because no one had ever taught me the importance of knowing my whole body. No songs had been sung, no initiation had taken place.

Yet I now converse with her. She is more than an organ. My womb is her own entity inside my body. This body that houses so much: all the different archetypes, personalities, quirks, and emotions. There are all the stories, scars, and muscle memory, along with my instincts, desires, and pleasure.

Not to mention my exertion, my strength, and my imagination.

***

'Head, shoulders, knees and toes, knees and toes…'

Lying in bed, exhausted and unnerved, I suddenly smile. I surrender to the words of the song and my attention scans down my body.

There is a beauty in naming the parts of my body. It takes me home and it brings me into the present moment. It lets me know I'm alive. Now, I expand the list to include thighs, arms, fingers, belly, heart, ears, nose, and womb – always my womb.

Staying in Touch

Catherine Cronin

Catherine Cronin

For a while there, I was very in touch with my body. It was me and it against the world. Or, at least, the small tumorous world that was crowding out healthy tissue in my breast. That world had moons in my armpits and a satellite near my lung, so the gravitational pull of it was immense. It weighed me down in a way that my obesity had not done before (though I thought it had because I thought about it *a lot*). I did not talk about the obsession with weight back then because it was boring and revealing. Besides, who needs to listen to the woes of an overfed, self-sabotaging misery guts?

Cancer, though, gives you permission to overshare. Well, maybe you are not given permission so much as you take it. You do it. You talk about it or you die. The doctors need to know everything going on in your body. So, every day you take stock, making an inventory of all the new pores, sores, and snores. You are forced to spend a lot of time with yourself naked, physically and emotionally, acquainting yourself with parts of your body you have never talked to before. Really listening. And the parts that you hid from strangers out of faux modesty are laid bare for all to see. The shame of cellulite, stretchmarks, and a big belly replaced by pointed fear and desperation. People strive for dignity in dying not dignity in treatment. You come to terms with that early on.

Back then, it helped to think of myself as a machine. The disconnect from flesh and sinew was a comfort and shielded my mind from destruction on days when my body had to be poisoned and pricked into health. I could float above the engine of me like some spectral guardian, removed from the damage, free to repeat affirmations to the pipes and coils. 'You can do this. Everything will be fine.'

However, in reality, I had no detached ethereal glamour. I was more like a pudgy stoker, sweltering in the heat of a tiny carriage, working flat out to shovel coal and speed the locomotive to the finish. Destination: remission.

In those early days of sweet oblivion, I did not know that my destination was different. Like a budget airline, it was more destination-adjacent.

I quickly learned that life-threatening illnesses are holistic. They attack everything – the head, the body, and the soul. Oh, and they break your heart too. Yes, heartbreak is inevitable. My first session of chemotherapy killed half of the main tumour in my breast, but it came with a nasty side effect: plummeting white blood cells. My immune system could not handle the crash and, eventually, some anonymous bacteria invaded my pores, landing me in the emergency room. My condition was on a knife's edge. I remember looking at my reflection and thinking, 'I can't do this. Everything's not fine.' I felt like it would save everyone a lot of work if I just faded away there and then. I had treated my own body so poorly over the years that I felt undeserving of the morphine and the broad-spectrum antibiotics they were going to use to save me.

Catherine Cronin

It is a dark moment I return to often. I even wrote it into a play and performed that moment on stage again and again. I still cannot believe I was so hopeless. The only thing that saved me was the sight of my anxious husband trying to process the intensity of the emergency. And it has taken me a long time to admit – accept even – that I did it for him and not for myself. In my hour of need, I did not rally for my own body.

Maybe that is not important. The important thing is, I *did* rally. I threw myself into healthy eating and exercise on the days I could. I walked the woods and learned to breathe. My doctor set me up with a psychotherapist who helped me navigate the treatment. For the first time in my life, I was in touch with the physical side of me. I envisioned myself whole. Of course, this had its obstacles (a mastectomy, a brief bout with thyroid cancer, and an ovariectomy), but I worked hard to sustain this new relationship between myself and my body.

The most glorious period of this brief bond was the one that lay between post-treatment and pre-plague. I was still on sick leave, writing my first play, and starting to feel strong again. I went to London for a solo trip a year to the day of my diagnosis. Crossing Waterloo Bridge, I soaked up the freedom and possibility of the city, conscious of the vital surgical scars beneath my shirt and the thicker hair on my head moving with the breeze. Once across, and inside the lobby of the National Theatre, I gave myself a quick little hug in a quiet corner. This is my therapist's trick. A moment of gratitude I should show my body for getting me through a deadly illness.

I was at the theatre to see Brian Friel's masterpiece, *Translations*. The play opens with the character of Sarah struggling to speak her name, thus introducing identity, communication, and alienation as major themes. It was the perfect piece to see in that moment as the characters struggled to define themselves in a colonised culture. Cancer had been my coloniser. I had to learn a whole new way to communicate and redefine myself in the wake of its invasion. Translating the lifelong disparate languages of my body and mind was fraught with miscommunication but also with possibility and the opportunity to hear something new. I came away from the theatre reminded that I would have to work hard to maintain my new mind-body equilibrium. That was December 2019.

My return to my job after treatment coincided with news reports of a contagious disease originating in China. Suddenly, everyone was stockpiling dry carbs and/or getting fit. I was doing both. Being immunocompromised, I was terrified. Or at least, I thought I was. I had no idea what real terror felt like, but I would soon learn.

I got a text message from one of my best friends, Karen, back in Ireland. She had leukaemia. It was bad. Really bad. I longed to hug her, even though she wasn't really one for hugging. We did not know then, but she would not see the end of lockdown. In spite of her confidence, mental strength, and diligence in looking after her body, her life was cut short. And because of the pandemic, most of her family and friends never saw her in person from the moment of diagnosis to the moment she slipped away.

Karen was the strongest woman I knew, which was great, but not what our friendship was built on. She had a wicked sense of humour and, like all great friends, loved when we had a marathon slagging match. The darker, the better. Cancer did not dull our skills in that regard. Not until the end. Then every laugh was laced with unsaid fear and pain.

Catherine Cronin

We streamed her funeral online that autumn and watched as they buried her in the graveyard of her local church. It was surreal. It all felt so *un*-physical. I had had no physical contact with her for her entire illness and now I was expected to accept that her body was lifeless and forever settled in the ground. It felt unnatural. She had nurtured me when I was ill and visited me when I had my mastectomy. The first time she saw me without breasts, she instantly put me at ease, and she was instrumental in helping me build a confident relationship with my new state of flat-chestedness.

When she got sick, I felt useless. I suspect many who knew her felt the same, as were the many others who were distanced from their own loved ones during the pandemic. I have lived the life of a distant family member for over a decade, ever since I moved from Ireland to Switzerland. But I could always get home before. Lockdown changed all that. There is no replacement for physical togetherness. I have thought about that a lot over the last couple of years.

About six months after my friend's death, my mother-in-law, Joan, passed away suddenly from a heart attack. She was six days away from getting a pacemaker, a procedure that had been postponed because of you-know-what. Just a few days prior, my husband had been planning to finally see her in person after months of restrictions. When he did get to make his trip in person, she was lying peacefully in her coffin.

I had arranged it with the funeral director for him to see her first at the wake. He needed time alone with her. He cried when he saw her in the flesh, tiny and vulnerable, so unlike the strong matriarch we had known. Her fingernails were painted with the pink Chanel polish he had gifted her. When we were alone, he asked me if it would be ok to touch her. I smiled and nodded. My own mother worked in a nursing home for years and has instilled in me a respect for the dead, removed from fearful remoteness. I suppose that was why he asked me.

He held her polished hand and sobbed. Over the course of the wake, he would periodically go and take his Mam's hand in lieu of an absent hug. Even though he was forty-eight and, even though she was lifeless, there was comfort in those last touches. Sadness was there too, of course, but there was also a nurturing and a savouring of the moment. This was the last time their physical bodies would ever be together. It was a stark contrast to the experience we had had with Karen.

On that same trip back to Ireland, we visited Karen's grave for the first time. I heaved angry, disbelieving sobs all the way back in the car. How could she be there? How was I getting away with surviving? How was that fair? How was I ok when I had never been as careful? How was I allowed to go on when the relationship I had with my body was so much worse than the one Karen had with hers? People say it's survivor's guilt but, with me at least, there is a lot more to this self-centred criticism.

The body positivity movement left the likes of me behind. That is not a fair statement, I know. It suggests I am owed something and that this abstract social effort is a sentient being. That is ridiculous, but I do feel bereft of a movement that speaks to me. I feel ashamed writing this down for anyone to read. It probably smacks of judgement, but there is none. This is an internalised conflict. I don't want to shame anyone – I am just being honest about how I feel.

Beauty is sizeless and loving the skin you're in is affirming, but I am not talking about beauty when I refer to my muddled feelings. The fact is, I do not feel healthy or even comfortable being overweight. You know that feeling when you've been in the water for ages and you have to leave the bliss of weightless floating behind and hoick yourself back to dry land? You become keenly aware of your heaviness and the pull of gravity, right? That is how I feel most of the time, especially when my weight is out of control. There has to be a way of talking about health and obesity without people feeling ashamed or embarrassed or dismissed as being perfectly fine the way they are.

Of course they are and of course I am, but the reality is, I struggle to fit in MRI machines and I am always a couple of centimetres away from asking for an extension belt on airplanes. And, yes, I know that there is a whole conversation to be had about the fairness of engineering and the 'averaging' of sizes when it comes to accommodating what industries have measured as 'normal' for the general population. But it still makes me feel bad. How could it not?

It makes me worry about the state of my health. I list off all the things that are now tipping the balance in favour of ill health: excess visceral fat, high blood sugar, hypertension, varicose veins, clogged arteries, etcetera, etcetera. I get anxious and my stomach knots and, to stop feeling the knots, I eat. I eat to unknot. I eat to feel stuffed. I eat to feel something else other than worry. I eat when I am stressed by the climate, the job, the fill-in-the-blank. Vicious, isn't it? This is a cycle I have wrestled with since childhood.

Now, add cancer into the mix. Then, a pandemic. And finish it off with grief.

It would be easy to blame my primogeniture rights to leftovers and my family's clean-all-the-plates approach to mealtimes. It would be easy to blame the society I grew up with that shamed me and my peers into feeling chronically bad about our bodies (easy and justified). It would be easy to blame myself… or at least it has been. Where will that blame get me? Where has it got me? Well, back to where I was before cancer.

Intellectually, I know that I need a better relationship with my body, but sometimes the knots distract me from those rational thoughts. I turned forty a few months ago and since then I have received some important lessons concerning the vocabulary I use, especially when I talk to myself.

The first instance occurred when I read a random online comment that cancers like mine should be called *chronic*, rather than terminal. I had cancer and have the BRCA2 gene, so I live with cancer's scythe lurking perpetually over me. However, though terminal cancers exist, my cancer does not have to be one of them. That shift in vocabulary really helped me. I am no longer as afraid of those potential carcinogenic colonisers in my body and I am listening to my therapist and not living my cancer anymore.

Then, the second lesson came with the word *fat*. A good friend of mine told me I should stop referring to myself as 'F. A. T.', making sure to mouth out the spelling almost wordlessly as she said it to me. Of course, she was right, but I didn't fully get the tiptoeing around the word. Then, serendipitously, I was listening to a podcast with Marian Keyes where she mentioned, in passing, how great it was that younger women were no longer using the slur *fat*. It was treated like a swear word, or worse, an offensive term of attack. There you go. Another part of the movement I missed. I need to read more or maybe just have more meaningful conversations with the women in my life. I should do both and really listen.

Catherine Cronin

The final piece of vocabulary was a German word, courtesy of my therapist. It was the word *Gelassenheit*. He translated it for me in our session to *serenity*.

Serenity. That is what I had been yearning for.

I had it. I did. Back during my gruelling chemo sessions. Back on Waterloo Bridge. Back before the loss and the hurt. What is more, I had seen it a couple of weeks before he tutored me on *Gelassenheit* when I was home in Ireland for my goddaughter's Christening, though it was her serenity and not my own.

She arrived at the church with her mother, calm and dressed in white. She lasted well in the stifling heat but eventually, cried to be relieved of her layered Christening gown – the same gown I had worn forty years previously. I thought about how we are all born with our Freudian ids in the driving seat. We cannot do anything but listen to our bodies and advocate for our physical needs – with noisy and messy results, of course, but even still!

Somewhere along the way, I lost that ability to advocate for my own body. Remarkably, cancer returned that to me and it was a powerful and motivating way to live. I have a renewed desire to seek serenity, stop living my cancer, and lose the self-slurring. The words I say to myself have meaning and undermine my ability to stay in touch with my body. I am sure I will need reminding of that often.

For a healthier now, I will take on the world with my body, even if sometimes that world is the negative one I built inside my head. I will hug, be hugged, and self-hug because the pull to that physical connection is immense. More than that, it is necessary, and you never know when that last hug is happening. I will learn the languages of my body and soul, careful to translate the meaning of their needs – listening, not just to understand them, but to maintain and stay in touch with them across any distance of time or space.

I suppose, as long as I stay committed to doing all this, there is still hope that I can crowd out those negative thoughts and, at long last, give my relationship with my body a real go of it.

Doctor Face: A Facelift Story

Kay Redrup

Kay Redrup

I never thought I'd have a facelift. I'll grow old gracefully, I told everyone.
    Like fuck I will.
    It wasn't vanity that took me on this journey. At the ripe age of sixty, it wasn't the need to have sex with someone other than myself, nor was it peer pressure. Instead, it was an innate need to recognise myself again. The woman I saw in the mirror simply wasn't me. She was bloated and her upper eyelids tired, making the shading of her eye shadow look ridiculous. Her high cheekbones were now her lower jawline, and her chin? Well, there wasn't one. The tip of it had joined itself with her neck and, from the side, she looked like a pelican.

'I want my jawline back,' I demanded from the mirror. With each passing week, my confidence declined, not because I considered myself ugly but because I didn't know who I had become. It did not match the person inside: the one that was fearless, opportunistic, nurturing, and rebellious.

My friend Claudia, a woman far less vain than myself but with a similar receding jawline, said, 'We have to do something.' And thus our search began. She picked the first doctor in our journey of many.

'We pull back the skin of the chin and neck to the side, and voila, you have your chin back,' the first doctor announced proudly. As his large hands pulled the loose folds of my face upwards beyond my ears, I briefly saw my old self before he let go and my face flapped back into place.

'He's not cheap,' Claudia smirked, 'but he's good-looking.' I'm not sure why that mattered to us. Was it a case of beauty recognising beauty? I have no idea, but we are shallow that way.

'I'm not happy with him. He's a smoker.'

'How'd you know?'

'I could smell his fingers.'

'Why does it matter?'

Unlike me, Claudia had never smoked, so she would not understand my concern. 'It matters a lot.' I was a recovering smoker, having puffed away twenty-four years of my life, and I knew all too well the power of addiction. There is little understanding for anyone's comfort when the body cries out for the drug.

'Imagine the surgery is taking a little longer than he envisaged. He might hurry things along because he needs to have a smoke!'

They say it's easier to stop heroin than nicotine. I'd say that the very fact that you don't have to relinquish smoking when entering the AA programme must say something about this gateway drug.

'It's a dealbreaker for me.'

For two years, we went in search of the perfect surgeon and, during that process, we learned how to narrow down our hunt to someone we trusted. We're talking about our faces, after all, something we have to wear every single day. We certainly didn't want to have the stretched lizard look or that startled caught-in-the-headlights rabbit look.

'You can't just do your chin,' said the doctor. 'It's like decorating the bottom part of your house and not the rest of it.'

He had a point. Suddenly, with the words of doctor number two, we learned that our chin lift would require nothing less than a full lift.

'Deep plane surgery,' another told us. *What the hell was that?* We tried not to squirm as he explained how he would cut into the muscles of our faces and reshape them before pulling the skin over. 'If you just stretch the skin, then it's going to make your face different. After all, you've lost contour over the years, and the face will start to fall soon after.'

'I like this doctor,' Claudia said. Despite his honesty, he was charming and he spoke with flair and confidence. He was also good-looking and didn't smoke.

'I'm not sure.'

'What are you not sure about? He doesn't smoke.'

'He trained privately.'

'What!'

'Did you see his diplomas on the wall? He went to private medical school. He didn't earn his place by passing state exams together with the top one percent. He got here with money. I want the doctor who works on our faces to have earned his merits working with burn and accident victims at a government hospital.'

'Oh good grief. You're hard to please. And you want one cheap!'

Claudia wasn't wrong there. Was I delaying this because deep down I didn't want to do it? Was I hoping my face would miraculously lift itself? I wasn't sure, but I was aware that I was finding reasons not to do it.

'We want to look natural. We don't want my mouth ends to start near our ears, and we don't want our skin stretched so taut it looks paper thin,' we told doctor number five.

'What's wrong with him?' asked Claudia as we left his surgery.

'Did you see the decor of his office? He's definitely no artist.'

The months passed. In between, we discussed Botox and threading, but I saw no point in either. Threading sounded horrendous. The thought of someone doing a runner stitch under my skin and then pulling it didn't fill me with a belief that the benefits after all that agony and angst would last longer than a year. I felt I had missed the boat with Botox as I didn't mind my wrinkles and it would do little to lift my turkey neck.

Then one day, Claudia sprang an ultimatum. 'I'm fed up with this searching. I need to get this done before spring starts. I've decided to go with doctor number one.'

Oh my god, the smoker!

'Claudia, give me one week to find our man.'

'No, I've had enough.'

'Let's have one more appointment then. If you don't like the next doctor I pick, then you go ahead with Dr Smoker and I will opt out.'

I set to work by writing a note to my knee doctor. My message should have read, 'I can barely do the stairs now and need a knee replacement. Can we arrange that please?' Instead, I wrote, 'Do you know any plastic surgeons by any chance?'

He sent me three choices. All doctors he had worked with. All had entered state medical school at the same time as he

Kay Redrup

had and at the same hospital. All three were under thirty-five. Feeling lucky, I picked the middle doctor on the list and made an appointment to meet Doctor Face.

His office was in an upmarket salubrious part of the city. You could hear the 'ka-ching' as you entered his building.

'It's got an elevator,' Claudia squealed, which was code for 'he's not going to be cheap.'

The first thing that struck us was the decor: it was stunning. Vibrant colours that I had not imagined would calm or invite me. Tabletop statues and old leather-bound books among tasteful pieces of his life and his interests – an old camera, folk dancing acrylics, a buddha, the hand of Fatima, and a bonsai plant, all of which spoke of taste, class and an artistic attention to detail.

Doctor Face, apart from being very good-looking, also had the body of someone who regularly went to the gym. Since he worked in the business of vanity, it made sense that he should represent it.

'No, I won't do deep plane surgery. It's too invasive. It cuts the muscle. You lose facial expression. It's what makes you look like you have had surgery. If you want natural, I suggest we do a mini lift,' he said and clicked open his TV presentation.

'See, we cut only the lower part of the face. Your bones have lost their density through age and we will rebuild the missing bone by using your natural fat. First, we will add more than you need, but in time, your body will absorb that and you will slowly emerge over months like a butterfly.'

His enthusiasm and innate confidence were nothing less than tantalising. 'We must do eyes too,' he said. 'We will remove the fat below them, cut into the lids and remove the excess skin. Then we will make a little incision above the eyebrow and raise it up with a stitch or two at the brow line. And we will do it all under local anaesthesia.'

Strangely, we hardly flinched when he said that. We were caught under his magic spell of the sleeping beauty kiss.

'I prefer local anaesthesia because I will ask you to move certain muscles of your face. This will ensure I don't cut where I shouldn't.' He made so much sense, I thought.

On our way down in the lift after leaving his office, we both spoke simultaneously. 'He's the one!'

We had finally found our man and his allure had been so great that we were ready to throw our life savings at him. Claudia agreed that she would have the surgery one week before me so I could take care of her, and then she could take care of me. He had filled us with such assurance that we felt like we were doing something more akin to eyebrow tattooing than lying on our backs for hours being cut and pulled. Our confidence was so high we even booked a wine tasting four days after my surgery. *Surely that's enough recovery time!*

On the day of reckoning, Claudia never faltered in her decision to go under the knife under local anaesthesia. I drove her to hospital and we were excited and jovial.

'I can't believe we are actually doing this!' she said.

'Neither can I! We haven't worked for a year. We haven't earned any money because of Covid. I need a knee replacement. But I know where our priorities lie!'

Our jokes continued as Doctor Face leaned in to draw lines all over her face. His energy and enthusiasm were seductive. I happily waved goodbye to Claudia as she was whisked away on a gurney for the five-and-a-half-hour procedure.

***

Kay Redrup

I am told that within half an hour of the cutting and splicing, Claudia told Doctor Face, 'My friend Kay can't do this. You have to put her under completely.'

Claudia then endured three hours before finally telling Doctor Face that she had had enough. He put her to sleep completely. When she awoke, her first words were, 'You must put Kay to sleep completely. She cannot do this.'

That day, I brought Claudia food, chocolate mousse and support. She looked horrendous. She told me little of what she had gone through, so as not to put me off, but enough to ensure I agreed to go under completely. Claudia knows all too well that I don't like pain. The fact that I gave birth to three children might make you wonder why I had not stopped at one, but that's another story.

Over the next few days, I wrestled with myself. I felt the peacock in me become a chicken. I was scared. Did I really want a chin so badly that I would subject myself to pain, discomfort, and the fear of death? The nostril intrusion of a Covid test required before surgery had already been causing me angst. Something that small had given me pause, so I wondered, was I ever going to be ready for something so major as elective surgery?

Claudia couldn't open her eyes properly for two days and sought relief from ice packs every hour. I explained to Doctor Face my fears about how I had lost a school friend to vanity some years before. She had gone to a top Beverly Hills surgeon for a facelift. When she woke up from surgery, she was gibbering in a foreign language, then raced to the roof, stripped herself naked and jumped off.

'If I start speaking another language, strap me down,' I insisted.

Kay Redrup

As the days passed, I tried to find the balance on my scales of indecision. On the one hand, there was the weight of vanity, and on the other, the weight of fear. As the hours passed, my left hand, full of fear, grew heavier. I wanted a new jawline less and less.

Then, out of the blue, another player entered the scales and kicked vanity and fear out of my hands: friendship. Claudia and I had embarked on this journey together for two years ago and we would do this together. We had visited numerous surgeons and clinic specialists offering alternatives and probed them with questions. We had talked endlessly about what we had learned, what we should do, what we could afford and why we wanted to do this. We were bound in our search for ourselves. And for me to not go through with it was to stop before we'd completed our journey. I owed it to our friendship.

Claudia was in no shape to sit with me when it was my turn. Her recovery was slow. I believe the trauma of her surgery played a big part in it, but without her having martyred herself, it might have been me, awake in the operation theatre, and frankly I simply could not have handled it.

Claudia, ever mindful of our pact, dragged herself to be with me when it was my turn. She was the one person who had seen my soul raw and had listened to my insecurities. She knew that there was great depth in my shallowness. Her still purple and swollen face exhibited every reason why I shouldn't be doing this, but with just two sentences, she gave me back the courage and belief I so desperately needed.

'I wouldn't blame you if you decided not to go through with this. But I do know this: if you don't, you will regret it.'

With courage and excitement, I entered the operating theatre, ready to say hello to myself again.

A Suit of Armour

Natasha Cabot

Natasha Cabot

There is very little difference between a suit of armour and a suit of fat. Both serve as a form of protection. One protects a person from slings, spears, and arrows, while the other protects a person against heartache or misplaced trust. Suits of armour have fallen out of fashion over the years, but the suit of fat still exists. It is far more effective than its metallic counterpart.

My primary reason for donning my armour of fat is simple – it is for self-protection. Yes, over the years people have made disparaging or hateful comments, but those are easily ignored or forgotten. I can dig deep into my well of unearned arrogance and tell myself that I am better than 'those people' who love to insult. I am smarter. I always have been far more intelligent than the idiots whose insults roll off their tongues as easily as carbs flow down my gullet. But fears of a broken heart or of abandonment nestle deep within the marrow of my sturdy, stout bones. It creeps around the sinew of musculature, and it bobs and weaves throughout the myriad yellow fat cells that gather in lumps and bumps throughout my body. The fear squeezes me like a lard-stuffed anaconda until I can barely breathe. Being fat affords me protection from the pitfalls of falling madly, deeply, passionately in love and of ever being abandoned. Though I tend to think of myself as the fattest person in the room or, indeed, the world, I am what I call 'Goldilocks' fat: not fat enough for chubby chasers, yet fat enough to repel. For quite a long while, it worked. Until suddenly it didn't.

Now I plod around trapped inside a corpulent body I despise because I am a fearful person.

It gets lonely, living with fear. Fear is terrible company, though at first it seems to soothe. It convinces you to barricade yourself within yourself so no one can ever, ever hurt you. It promises to keep you safe. 'No one will ever hurt you if you listen to me,' it whispers. And, like a fool, you believe it. So, you do as it says and then twenty years later you find yourself still safe yet utterly miserable. Fear doesn't make jokes or hold your hand. Fear is anxiety-inducing and full of what-ifs.

The calendar not only bears witness to the years spent in a perpetual foetal position, praying to be more invisible each day, it watches as you swallow chips, cookies, pizza, and ice cream with malevolent glee. With prayers granted, 99% of people cannot see you, but your misery is ever-growing and never seems to end. Fear is the perfect abusive bastard: smart enough not to leave bruises on the skin but diabolical enough to scar the hell out of the inside.

Keeping myself fat over the past twenty years has been a profound mistake. I think of things I have missed or failed to enjoy. I have been attacked by severe bouts of anxiety when travelling, fearful that I won't be able to fit in a plane's seat, or I will sit next to someone who surreptitiously photographs me and puts me on social media with horrifying captions like, 'Why didn't they make this lard ass buy two seats? I'm dying here!' Smiley face emoticons following in the wake of a cruel phrase.

I missed the chance to swim in Salinas de Pedra de Lume, a salt crater in Cape Verde because I didn't want people to see me in a swimsuit. I have wandered around streets in Dublin, London, and Prague terrified that someone will see me and shake their head in disgust. I visited a concentration camp in Czechia, and I could feel everyone's eyes on me. I knew they were thinking I could do with a few good months in such a camp. Then I immediately felt guilty for letting something so horrific become all about me.

For the past twenty summers, I have refused to wear shorts for fear someone will call me turkey legs or poke my dimples of cellulite, which cascade beautifully on my thighs like a vast constellation in the sky.

I haven't had sex in forever because of my weight. I am ashamed to let a man see me naked. Yes, fat women regularly get laid, but to quote Groucho Marx, 'I refuse to join any club that would have me as a member.' My innate snobbery forbids me from being with anyone who 'settles' for me.

I know I'm the problem. I have always been mortified by myself, even when I was thinner. I never had any self-esteem to begin with, even though I falsely believe that I am smarter than many people. When a person has no self-esteem, it is easy to be cruel to oneself. Abusing my body by making it larger was a form of self-punishment that I never needed to go through. There are happy fat people out there who live amazing lives, and I'm proud of them, but I'm not one of them – and I'm ashamed to say so. I wish I could be, but I can't. I don't want to live with something I inflicted upon myself.

Now I realise that my fat, my suit of artery-clogging armour, is stifling me. It wears me down to the point I can't even keep my shoulders straight. They slump forward like two exhausted potatoes. I'm tired of always being tired. Lugging around seventy or eighty extra pounds gets more difficult with each passing year.

I am in therapy, currently learning to tolerate myself. I am sure love will come later, but it will take time. Right now, tolerate is the best that I can do. It is a long, difficult, annoying process, but I need to heal myself. The only way I can do that is to shed the reminder of my self-hate. Gradually, I am pulling off the armour, pound by pound. I cannot get the past twenty years back no matter how much I want to – those are gone forever. However, I can do my best to enjoy the next twenty, thirty, forty, or fifty years. I do not intend to do it inside a prison of my own making. There are so many things I want and need to do. I want to sail, hike, be active. I want to return to Cape Verde and swim in Salinas de Pedra de Lume. And though some people can enjoy those things within an extra-large body, I can't. Perhaps I am weak for wanting to conform to societal norms – so be it. If I am, I apologise to my larger-bodied brethren and sistren, but I can say this: I have been fat, and I have been thin. I know which one makes me feel better.

Sex Ed: Mormon Edition

Hillary Jarvis

Hillary Jarvis

Since my dad is a doctor, you'd assume that anatomy and sexual education would be a normal part of my everyday life. And to some extent, it was. My dad often regaled us with his harrowing tales of doctor life: the time he pulled a frog out of a vagina (she has no idea how it got there) or the time a romantic couple used strawberry jelly as a lubricant ('It's jelly!') or the time he had to call the CDC to confirm whether a human can get rabies from biting a rabid bat (turns out you cannot). However, he never talked about body parts or what you do with those body parts. At least not with me.

My parents love to tell the story of how they educated my oldest brother about sex.

'When he was five,' my mom chuckled, 'Ben asked me about how babies are made. I told him to talk to Dad about it, and being a doctor, Dad gave him a direct, anatomically correct definition of sex.' More chuckling. 'Soon all the parents in the neighbourhood were asking Dad to give the sex talk to their kids.'

Which was great for the neighbourhood kids and for my brother, but not for me.

The first time I remember talking about anatomy was in maturation class when I was in fifth grade. All the fifth grade girls and I huddled into a classroom where a beaming, bright-eyed woman tried to convince all of us that bleeding out of our hoo-ha (because we wouldn't *dare* say the word vagina) was something to celebrate and applaud. They handed each of us a plastic bag with a pad wrapped in pale yellow filmy paper and a pamphlet celebrating the joys of womanhood. It was horrifying.

In case I wasn't already embarrassed enough by my nether regions, my mother took me on a trip – just the two of us – to Toronto, Canada. Somewhere on the road between our voyage on the Maid of the Mist through Niagara Falls and our ascent to the CN Tower, my mom reiterated to me the steps of becoming a woman (pubic hair and breasts and periods, oh my!). It was the first and last time we ever talked about *that*.

When my period started at the age of fourteen, I was away at camp. Luckily, I had already been trained to bring a hearty supply of pads with me everywhere I went, so I didn't even call home about it. I balled up my bloody panties, peeled off the liner, and began my monthly journey of shame. I eventually told my mom about my period, who from that moment on would discreetly leave packages of pads on my bed. We never talked about it again.

I did, however, talk about it with my college boyfriend, Brett. One night, he asked, 'Why do you have periods? It's not like I bleed once a month!'

To which I replied, 'I don't actually know.' And I didn't.

From then on, I simply avoided swimming any time I had my period. Since I had been trained to never talk about, look at, touch, or even acknowledge my 'private parts,' I had no idea how to use a tampon, and trying to figure it out seemed complicated and, frankly, gross. *That area* was off-limits – at least until I was married.

This method of avoidance worked until I was nineteen when my grandpa paid for an incredible trip for his children and grandchildren through the Grand Canyon. It was a week of rafting, floating, hiking, and swimming. Lucky me, it was also the week of my period.

Do you know how hard it is to watch your entire family splashing around in the Colorado River while you sit on the side because Aunt Flo came for a visit? I was embarrassed and isolated and ostracized, all because of my feminine parts. My dutiful sister, who is three years younger than me, tried to help. In an act of true self-sacrifice and total humiliation, she demonstrated on herself how a tampon works (being sisters, our periods were synced up). In the middle of the Grand Canyon, as we hid behind a rock formation just out of view of our cousins, aunts, and uncles, she slowly grabbed that dangling string between her legs and pulled out her saturated, used tampon right in front of me. It was simultaneously an act of true sisterhood and the most disgusting moment of my young adulthood. I couldn't even understand what was happening. Where had that tampon been? Where was it coming from?

If that weren't enough, she then tried to help me put a tampon in myself.

'Maybe try pinching it with your fingers here… angle it this way… push here. Can you
squat down a little more? Maybe if I just…' We must have looked like a cross between a two-headed octopus and a screeching monkey: a combination of limbs twisting, tangling, and flailing and spontaneous screams as the tampon jabbed into my lady parts again and again.

Eventually, we both gave up and I wore a pad in my swimsuit into the river. Within moments, my pad dislodged from its location, quickly floated away in the current, and has probably either ended up in one of those giant floating islands of trash in the ocean or has killed a sea turtle. Either way, it was a disaster.

Just a year and a half later, when I got engaged, I realised that I needed to finally figure myself out. I vaguely understood what sex was thanks to a *How Things Work* book my parents bought me as a pre-teen. I kind of knew what a penis looked like, thanks to a crudely drawn image that my college boyfriend made for me, but I really didn't understand the logistics. I found myself wondering all sorts of things: how did people of different heights have sex when their 'special parts' didn't line up? How did men find the right hole when I couldn't even find it? How would I know how to deal with a penis in me when I couldn't even get a tampon in?

I should have asked all these questions at my pre-marital gynaecologist visit. I should have had my doctor show me how to use a tampon. I should have done some self-exploration and learned my own body more fully.

Instead, as I sat loosely wrapped in a worn, flowery hospital gown at the doctor's office, I panicked. My heart started racing. My fingers and toes began to turn blue and lose blood flow. All of my Mormon sex education came flooding back.

You see, Mormon sex education is absent at best and harmful at worst.

Every Mormon girl gets the same set of lessons about sex: don't talk about it. Talking about it will lead you to do something about it. As a woman, your job is to ignore it. Don't touch yourself. Don't arouse yourself. Your body is not your own and you are not a sexual creature. Your body is a gift from God to your future husband. He is the only one that should be *there*.

Furthermore, as a woman, you are responsible for not only keeping yourself sexually pure but also keeping the boys around you pure. Don't be a Bathsheba, tempting David with your body. Be pure, be modest, be clean. If a boy ends up committing a sexual sin with you, it is 100%, without a doubt, absolutely your fault. He can't help it; he's a boy. But you – you know better.

To emphasise this, Mormon young women are subjected to a variety of fear-inducing, soul-damning lessons.

First, there's the cupcake lesson. The Sunday school teacher brings a cupcake to class and asks if anyone wants it. Of course, everyone does. But then she licks it, leaving behind an oozing, glistening trail of saliva on the otherwise perfect mound of frosting. Of course, no one wants the cupcake now.

'And that,' she says, 'is what happens to you when you commit a sexual sin. You become a licked cupcake. And no one will want you.'

Then there's the chewed gum lesson. The Sunday school teacher brings in a piece of gum for every member of the class. All the young women happily pop the gum into their mouths and begin smacking away as the teacher discusses the seriousness of sexual sin. At the end of class, the teacher tells each young woman to give her gum to her neighbour.

'You mean you don't want somebody else's chewed gum?' she asks slyly. 'Well, then don't become chewed gum yourself.'

Finally, there's the hammer and nail lesson. 'Committing a sexual sin,' says the teacher, 'is like hammering this nail into a board.' Bang, bang, bang! 'And even though you can repent,' she says as she wriggles the nail out, 'there will always be a mark on you.' She points to the giant hole, a symbol of how imperfect you will always be.

As I sat there in that doctor's office, I asked nothing. I talked about nothing. I declined a pelvic exam. I assumed that sex would be natural, godly, and beautiful once I was married. That's what I'd been told.

Plus, I felt like I had done all the right things to be ready for *sex*.

My fiancé and I took a Marriage Prep class the semester we got engaged. (Is that a normal class at college? Or just at BYU?) I honestly remember nothing about it except for the lesson about sex. Our professor, a happily married, middle-aged white male, stood at the front of the room and proudly displayed a Nike swoosh on the screen. 'There's only one thing you need to know about sex,' he proclaimed.

Ok, this is good! I thought. I rapidly scribbled down 'SEX' in all caps on my lined notebook page.

'When your husband wants sex, remember the Nike symbol. Just do it!'

Just do it! Definitely the key to romantic, fulfilling, intimate sex.

Hillary Jarvis

My fiancé and I read a book about sex just months before our wedding. It was called *And They Were Not Ashamed: Strengthening Marriage through Sexual Fulfillment* by Laura M. Brotherson. I was simultaneously fascinated and terrified. It was the first time I learned about orgasms (your legs shake?) and the clitoris (I had to look up where that was in my high school sister's biology book). There was so much information – pages and pages and pages of sexual knowledge. Being a perfectionist and a straight-A student, I had no idea how I was going to memorize and then perform up to the standards that the book suggested, but at least I had a basis for what was to come.

Most importantly, I did finally learn to put a tampon in a few weeks before I got married. It happened one afternoon as I stood in a stall on BYU's campus with my cousin tentatively coaching me outside the door ('How are you doing? Did you get it in?'). I still had never touched myself *there*. I couldn't even locate my own clit, but I at least knew where my vagina was.

Believe me, that didn't really help on my wedding night.

Waiting for Weight Loss (and Other Things)

Adrian Slonaker

Adrian Slonaker

It's 6:41 a.m. on sunny Vancouver Island at the far western edge of Canada, and I am about to indulge in an appropriately summery breakfast: a chilled can of locally-produced Sparkmouth strawberry sparkling water containing zero calories (or kcals or kJoules), zero carbs and zero fat. I beam at my self-discipline, compensating for my disgusting lack of control last night in the form of an iced halvah coffee, two falafel wraps, and a turmeric cookie. I practically quiver with the shame more appropriate for someone who'd just firebombed an orphanage. I may not eat for the rest of the day, or if I do, possibly something light – under 300 calories – before bedtime so that I'll be able to sleep without waking up from food dreams or annoying hunger pangs. And yet, as a broad-shouldered, middle-aged person who passes as male and looks more like a line backer or rugby player than how individuals with eating disorders are typically portrayed in the media, I trudge through day-to-day life with my struggle invisible and unsuspected. Few people perceive how I wince when I'm called 'big guy'. Perhaps

Adrian Slonaker

even fewer realise my squeals of delight when I squeeze into jeans that are closer to what I deem an 'appropriate' size.

There is an episode of the sci-fi series *The Twilight Zone* called 'Judgment Night' in which a Nazi is doomed to relive, night after night for eternity, the horror experienced by the passengers of the British ship that he and his U-boat crew had fired upon during the war. Similarly, almost every night for decades, I have felt guilty for not being vigilant enough about my weight – for how I dare to present myself to others in a way that pollutes the aesthetic landscape of society.

My mother's side of the family is known for blossoming into plumpness in middle age. My paternal line, however, is a different story, overflowing with individuals who are slim for a few years but then, regardless of era, sex, diet, activity level or location, explode into obesity between the ages of four and eight, thus initiating a lifelong struggle. When my late Auntie Penny was in her forties, after her umpteenth diet (this time a strict liquid plan), she could not drop below a certain weight no matter how hard she tried and despite her gaunt and ashen face. My mother, trying to be helpful, cooed, 'It's probably your body type. You're not meant to be pencil thin.'

My auntie practically wailed, 'But I want to be thinner!' I had never related to anyone else's words so closely. She never achieved her dream.

In my case, it occurred between the ages of seven and eight. Photos from the very early 1980s show that, despite being an avid swimmer and bike rider, I quickly underwent a radical enlargement as my young body betrayed me for the first but not the last time. As far as I know, I had not experienced a corresponding change in diet. My new look didn't go unnoticed as mean boys and mean girls in school commented on my size and my inability to run as fast or play team sports as well.

My maternal grandmother pointed at my teddy bear and declared that he and I both had pot bellies and that I should exercise more. It's astounding that, in the Mennonite faith, to which my family traditionally belonged and to which my grandmother had adhered all her life, young people cannot be baptised until the age of sixteen because, before that, they are thought to lack the maturity and discernment to make such a commitment. Yet here I was, under ten and supposed to be the master of my own biology and anatomy. To my parents' credit, though, they have rarely body-shamed me. My father, despite being a star football player in school, has been plagued with the same issues, as has my brother. Dad dieted as a child in the 1950s. He dieted as a young adult in the late 1960s. And he still diets as a senior citizen in the 2020s.

In addition to my jelly-like rolls of fat and wide thighs, I was becoming increasingly near-sighted (a gift from my mother's side of the family, as those people tend to require glasses at around the same age as my father's family balloon in size) and was prescribed the thick hideous glasses of that era. Furthermore, I inherited the overbite of my critical grandmother, and clunky silver braces were determined to be part of my future. While some people, as adults, look back at their childhood pictures with joy and/or conclude that their awkward phases were not as bad as they thought, I still look at my vintage photos with horror, amazed I was even able to leave the house looking as I did.

Fortunately, despite my appearance, I performed well academically and, in high school, hobnobbed with other honours students. Frequently labelled bookworms, nerds, or geeks, they seemed to be more accepting of me for my personality and my scholastic achievements, and I was able to make friends and even dated (although I did not have sex).

At university, however, the weight comments continued, either rudely ('you eat like a pig') or disguised as concern ('I can help you lose weight if you want'). In addition, by my late teens, it was becoming increasingly impossible to ignore my emerging sexual curiosities and desires. Complicating matters was the fact that, while I was attracted to women, I found that I was also drawn to men, usually even more deeply. My first kiss with a male friend in the darkness of my dorm room was electric.

Around the same time, my mother became a born-again Christian, and my father soon followed, creating a schism in my family. Weeks later, they found out about my queerness when Dad was snooping in my bedroom and found a letter I'd stupidly left on my desk long before I was ready for my parents to possess this information. They were not – and are not – accepting of it.

At the time, I was desperate to be loved and accepted, so shortly after my twentieth birthday, I embarked upon a strict diet of eating once every other day, accompanied by appetite suppressants. The plan worked, and the weight evaporated from my body relatively quickly. The positive feedback I received from others, more satisfied that I was inhabiting a more socially acceptable body than concerned about how I was achieving it, motivated me to continue to drop kilograms/pounds. Only when it was the middle of summer and I was still freezing, in addition to losing clumps of hair that never returned, did I figure I should tweak my weight loss approach. At the time, I figured that premature baldness was a small price to pay for the joy of thinness. After all, I could always wear hats.

Once I went off my rigid slimming regime, I boarded a carousel of bingeing, purging, cardio exercise, laxatives, and more over-the-counter diet pills and caffeine pills. Cigarettes entered the picture soon after. And though body fat was kept at bay for a while, the self-hatred was not. I cut my limbs with razors, wanting to transform emotional pain into something palpable and visible, since the physical hunger was not punishment enough for not looking the way I 'should'.

In fact, this insecurity was exacerbated by my awareness that, if the straight community is lookist and shallow, the queer male community is an exaggerated caricature of that behaviour. There's a reason why the expression 'straight thin but gay fat' exists. At this point, one of my friends became alarmed at my overall behaviour and notified the university authorities, who intervened. Even then, the clinician at health services noted down that I was suffering from 'exhaustion', explaining the diagnosis in the form of a question: 'Do you really want me to put down in your file that you have an eating disorder?' The mandatory short course of counselling, filled with unhelpful chatter and weak attempts at guidance, proved to be practically useless, much like the varying lengths of talk therapy that I'd turned to before and that I would eventually try again ('If at first you don't succeed…').

I graduated from university on time, but the body image struggles remained. Moving to a larger city, I explored this community further. Being young, thin and with fixed teeth and contact lenses, I attracted men. For the first time in my life, I was an object of sexual desire, and I relished the attention. I engaged in lots of sex, using it as the illusion of love and

Adrian Slonaker

acceptance that I did not feel elsewhere, either from my family or myself.

It was also a 'fuck you' to the past. It was a 'fuck you' to the girl in high school who told me that no one, not even her dog, would ever go out with me. It was a 'fuck you' to people who thought I was a nice, smart friend but clearly in the 'too gross to be sexual' category. Despite my promiscuity, I was terrible at longer-term relationships, in large part because I figured that, as attractive as I might seem now to some individuals, they would have likely rejected me if they'd known me before. In fact, one man, upon seeing a photo of me from high school, told me that I'd been a 'monster' but that now I was a 'muñeco' (Spanish for 'male doll').

Ultimately, however, I did develop a relatively healthy relationship with a woman called Carlene, who became my best friend and ultimately my wife. Also burdened with a history of weight and body image concerns, she saw and understood those issues in me. We listened to each other and propped each other up, and I stopped cutting myself. However, we also binged on food and then dieted together on numerous occasions. Although our marriage ended amicably a few years later, as it turns out that both of us thrive better when living alone, we are still close. We still support and enable each other.

Since my divorce, I have waded in and out of queer spaces, sometimes becoming involved with the bear community that tends to value, appreciate, and promote larger body types. Yet I am somewhat uncomfortable with the emphasis on looks here, too. And I still crave thinness; when I watch Mia Farrow on *Peyton Place*, I wish I had her bony, angular figure. I heard somewhere that people who wish to inhabit smaller bodies often do so because they feel vulnerable and wish to be taken care of, like children. As someone who is frequently overwhelmed by 'adulting', there may be some truth to that.

Somehow, paradoxically, when I punish my body, when I diet, I feel that I am letting the critics and assholes win. When I reject food, I feel like I'm validating the unkind words of schoolmates or the doctor who simply said, 'Well, you hide your weight well' after I'd lifted up my shirt to show him my visible ribs. That was my response to his request that I lose weight because I was on the wrong side of the BMI threshold. So maybe I am making some progress, which is what I suspected when Carlene and I undressed at a nude beach this year for the first time.

I recently celebrated my fiftieth birthday. That has brought up a new set of body image concerns related to ageing. As opposed to my ongoing problems with weight, hair (which I now dye), teeth (which have been shifting) and poor eyesight, I have been fortunate enough to have hassle-free skin that has aged slowly, despite my extended love affair with tobacco cigarettes (which ended on 8 June, 2010). As a drowning person might hang onto a lifeboat, I have clung to my skin's youthfulness with cleansers, exfoliants, sunscreens, and moisturisers, all of which feature a gamut of ingredients from Alaskan glacial water to snail slime. I have treated myself to facials, chemical peels, and microneedling. Last spring, I underwent my first round of Botox and Dysport injections. I am delighted by the vibrant smoothness, feeling that perhaps if I can look younger for longer, this will buy me time to finally be comfortable in my skin, at least for a while. I've been waiting for so long.

After reading a selection of my poems, a friend pointed out that many of them contain references to food. He found this to be strange and asked me about the reason. I hadn't noticed this trend, but he was correct. The obsession with eating (or not eating) runs deep. This observant friend also asked me, after I'd told him about my Botox treatment, why I'm so hung up on my external appearance. This essay might serve as an explanation.

In the late 2000s, like many other people, I signed up for Facebook and embraced the opportunity to reconnect with acquaintances from the past. I struck up a friendship with a schoolmate (let's call her 'Jennie') I hadn't known very well. On a blustery afternoon in November 2009, she wrote me a message apologising for not getting to know me sooner. She explained that because I was known as 'the fat kid' in elementary school, she wanted nothing to do with me at all. When I was a kid, I'd feared that people were simply dismissing me because of my looks, and, decades later, I learned it was true. Other Facebook users had apologised for the way they'd treated me, and I'd forgiven them, as it'd be absurd to demonise adults for their behaviour as kids. But those individuals had known me, interacted with me, and then decided they hadn't liked me. In some warped way, they had given me a chance. Not Jennie. I wanted to say, 'You must have terrible parents to teach you how to discriminate at such an early age.'

As Jennie had, with age, put on some weight, I was tempted to snipe, 'Given how you look now, karma's a bitch – and so are you!'

I didn't. I took the high road and simply replied, 'Well we were kids then. What matters is that we're friends now.' As soon as I pressed send, I sensed I'd been too kind to her. Our friendship later crumbled for unrelated reasons, and, thirteen years later, I still feel I let her off too easy.

Yours is Not the Only Erection in the Room

Bruce Loeffler

Bruce Loeffler

Early childhood sexual abuse marked my life and made sex a fraught and difficult terrain for me.

Childhood sexual abuse happens to a body already fully wired for sexual sensation and response, but to a boy who knows nothing about sex. It is terrifying and painful, because an adult man is not meant to put himself inside a very small boy. Childhood sexual abuse is an overwhelming event – a mix of pleasure and terror and pain. The young boy's mind dissociates, separating himself from his own body to remove him from the horror. It also erases the abuse from his memory each time like a shaken Etch-a-Sketch. The sexual abuse happens, but the boy does not know, does not remember.

It remains, however, unseen – in his body, in his nervous system, in his deep subconscious. It influences and invisibly controls *everything* that comes after.

I only discovered this erased memory at sixty-eight years old in the front row of a movie theatre while watching the graphic rape scene in *Boy Erased*. My body reacted and I *knew* that I'd been raped by a much larger person. That I was small and powerless to stop it. That it was terrifying and painful.

Only then did I begin to know my story: a story I did not choose for myself, but a life's journey that was chosen for me by others.

I know now that coming out as a gay man at twenty-six into the sex-first gay world of the seventies only compounded the sexual damage and insecurities from my childhood sexual abuse.

***

If you're a gay man having sex with another man, yours is *not* the only erection in the room. Comparisons are inevitable and everyone clocks it. I had an early boyfriend who referred to his own penis as 'Eveready' (like the battery brand) and to mine as 'Penlight.' I suspect he was thinking D-cells for his, and… what? Implying AAAs for mine? Although my penis *was* smaller, ours weren't all that different in size.

Those nicknames told me everything I needed to know about him – about his inflated sense of himself and his need to diminish others.

The average straight man does not see many erect penises in the flesh other than his own, except perhaps in a circle jerk as a teenager or in the locker room or the showers when someone gets semi-hard – after all, penises are notoriously independent. Maybe a walk on the wild side, once or twice, with another guy. Certainly, straight men see other erections in the exaggerated world of porn, which obviously skews large, but they know this, and the comparison isn't side-by-side.

If you're a straight man having sex with a cis woman, yours is the *only* erection in the room. You don't have to measure up against anyone else in bed. Of course, straight men can still be insecure. They can imagine that other men are better hung. They can worry they won't measure up to their female partners' previous lovers.

But actual side-by-side comparisons? Generally, straight men are spared this.

When I was in my mid-thirties, I made a list of all the men I'd slept with in order. I still remembered all their names, with one or two exceptions. There were seventy men on that list. I never counted again, but I was headed into a more settled period of long-term relationships, so I think the lifetime total couldn't be much above eighty-five. That number might seem shocking to some, but for a gay man in my age cohort, it is not large.

I was *not* in the fast lane of bathhouses and anonymous hook-ups or even one-night stands, per se. When I was picked up in a gay bar, I was looking for a life partner and trying to get to a second date.

Out of those eighty-five or so erections I've had in my hand, every other man I've been with had a larger penis, with only one exception – a man with an astonishingly pencil-thin three-inch erection.

All of this made me feel inadequate, and even defective. I was underhung and undesirable.

We didn't actually get our rulers out, so it was more of an impression, but it hurt nonetheless.

***

There have been a few recent meta-studies of penis size, with large datasets compiled from urology journal articles. Even so, there are substantially fewer published data for erect penises than for flaccid ones.

As it turns out, the official length measurement is consistently done by pushing the ruler in a bit at the pubic bone to eliminate the variability in fat pad thickness at the base of the penis. This is *exactly* what every guy does when he measures his own erection (and they've *all* done it). They push the ruler in to get that extra half inch, as I did, but as a standard measurement cited in the literature, it's totally legit!

Every man knows his penis size like he knows his shoe size. It's private information, guarded like a nuclear secret, never shared with other men.

The compiled data on penis length and girth can be plotted on bell curves. Based on 15,500 penises, the tops of those bell curves give the length and girth for the fiftieth percentile, or median penis, which I show below. Half of measured penises are larger than this, while half are smaller.

Erect length	13.1cm (5.51 in)
Erect girth (mid-shaft circumference)	11.7cm (4.61 in)
Flaccid length	9.16cm (3.61 in)
Stretched flaccid length	13.1cm (5.16 in)

It turns out there's a very high correlation (as above) between erect length and the length of a flaccid penis stretched to its maximum extension without excessive force, which means the stretched flaccid length is a good predictor for its erect length. This helps bolster the more limited length data for erect penises with the much larger dataset for flaccid ones.

Any penis can then be measured and compared to these bell curves, allowing it to be compared to 15,500 other penises.

For my penis, the data are:

Erect length	14cm (5.51 in)	65th percentile
35% of erect penises are longer than mine		
Erect girth	11cm (4.33 in)	25th percentile
75% of erect penises are thicker than mine		
Flaccid length	10.5cm (4.13 in)	80th percentile
20% of flaccid penises are longer than mine		
Stretched flaccid length	14cm (5.51 in)	65th percentile
This is the same data as for my erect penis, which is typical.		

My erection is not, then, actually shorter than most men, In fact, 65% of men have erect penises that are shorter than mine, although not necessarily by much. However, my erection is thinner than most. When I was thinking my penis was smaller than those of the other men I've had sex with, I was really sensing its overall mass. Since my erection isn't shorter but it *is* thinner, overall it looks less massive.

There's also the difference between 'show-ers' and 'grow-ers' to consider. Some men, the 'show-er's, generally carry more blood in their penises when flaccid, so the difference between flaccid and erect is not that great. They look impressive in the locker room. For other men, the 'grow-ers', their flaccid penises are quite reduced in size compared to their erections and may not look all that impressive in the shower.

I once had a friend whose flaccid penis was short and stout, nestled on top of his balls, just an inch or so in length. We once fooled around, and his penis grew, and kept growing, to a massive eight-inch erection. My jaw dropped. *Damn!*

From the above data, I know my flaccid length is substantially longer than most men, which means I'm a 'shower' and I can hold my own in the locker room. Other men have definitely noticed it, and a few gay men have tried to pick me up in the locker room. Naked and soft, I appear hung, but I don't grow that much from my soft state, so my erect penis appears smaller than many other erections.

Speaking of volume, the penis is a cylinder. Calculating the volume of a cylinder is the product of its cross-sectional area times its length ($V = \pi r^2 \times l$). A penis's erect volume can be calculated from its measured girth and its measured length. The penis girth (measured mid-shaft) is the circumference of a circle ($2\pi r$) from which you can calculate the penis radius (r), from which you can calculate its cross-sectional area (πr^2). Multiply this by its length (l) to get the penis volume.

The median erect penis volume, from the above tabulated data, is 8.68 cubic inches (142.3 cubic centimetres); mine is 8.21 cubic inches (134.6 cubic centimetres). My penis volume is 5.4% below the median.

To estimate where my penis fits on the bell curve for volume (though volume data for penises are *not* published), I could use the average of its girth percentile (25th) and its length percentile (65th), which is 45th percentile. Approximately 55% of penises are larger in volume than mine. So why don't urologists measure and publish penis volumes and put those on a bell curve? Volume is the essential factor in overall penis size, which is what men are really responding to when they assess whether they are well-hung or not.

How could you measure the volume of a penis or an erection? You could fill a graduated cylinder with (warm) water to a certain level. An erection inserted into the cylinder would displace a volume of water, which could be measured as the increase in water level in the cylinder. That would be the erect penis's volume.

I wonder if straight men would still be as anxious about their size if they knew that the average length of an unstimulated woman's vagina is 3 inches (7.62 cm) and its average opening is 1.14 inches (2.90 cm). The aroused vagina extends to an average length of 4.5 inches (11.4 cm). In either case, the median penis (5.16 inches, 13.1 cm) is longer than the average vagina.

For that matter, would gay men feel more secure about their size if they knew the average anal canal length is 1.73 inches (4.39 cm) and the average male rectal length is 4.7 inches (11.9 cm)? The prostate sits just behind the rectal wall, next to where the anus meets the rectum, so a three-inch finger (or penis) is enough to stimulate the sensitive nerves of the anus and long enough to massage the prostate.

The same is true for stroking the sensitive tissue of the vagina: a three-inch finger will do.

***

I obsessed about my penis for so long because I lived with a marked insecurity about my masculinity.

I was disempowered, disappeared, disembodied by early childhood rapes, which began when I was two or three. First by my grandfather, then by my older brother.

Bruce Loeffler

Men are supposed to be strong, able to protect themselves. Men are *not* supposed to be weak. When I was raped as a young child, neither flight nor fight was possible, so I froze, went completely passive. Then the abuse was less painful, over more quickly.

Men are supposed to be active in straight sex, they are *not* supposed be passive and take it up the butt.

And men are supposed to be athletic. *Not* uncoordinated. As a gentle, sweet kid with no eye-hand coordination, I sucked at team sports, was regularly humiliated in PE class.

And I was late to puberty, compared to other boys, so I was in the locker room with my tiny boy's penis, while my peers ran around with their man dicks. I shrank from their towel-snapping and proud display.

My mother – sodomized as a child by her father, the same serial-paedophile who later raped me – had an unacknowledged rage at men. She diminished and humiliated my father, my brother and me. She flirted and seduced, needed the sexual attention of men, including her own sons. Under sheer nylon nightgowns, she flaunted her perfect breasts, her triangle of pubic hair. Made us hard.

But she also often said to me, like a mantra, 'Sex is not my favourite sport.'

A seduction *and* a rejection. Groomed to be her surrogate spouse, but never taken to her bed. Covert incest without actual sex.

And unlike my jock brother, who looked just like James Dean, I was no athlete; if sex were a sport, I'd surely suck at that too.

Bruce Loeffler

My mother struggled with constipation, as I did – a reflexive clenching in response to anal rape to keep everything out, but which also kept everything in. She obsessed about defecation. Gave me regular enemas until I was ten or eleven. I even have an enema memory from when I was thirteen, but can that be right?

She made me strip and lie bare-ass-up on the bathroom floor, inserted the Vaseline-smeared nozzle hanging like a snake from the dull red enema bag, undid the clip. And water flooded into me sensuous and warm, until it hurt, really hurt, and the water kept coming.

My mother raped and humiliated me – naked on the bathroom floor, naked on the toilet, sweaty and chilled, dazed and empty. My mother inflicted her anger at men on me, and her enemas resonated with my other unremembered rapes.

My brother, nine years older also raped as a child by our grandfather, also abused by our mother before me – directed his rage at me. So much so that I thought he would kill me.
He pinned me down, tied me up, made me into his sex doll when I was five, six, seven, until he left for college when I was nine.

It was a way to reclaim his own masculine power, I suspect.

After my parent's divorce when I was ten, I lived alone with my mother while she continued to groom me as her spouse. She never dated anyone else: she had *me*. We vacationed together, like a couple, to tropical Caribbean isles, sometimes sleeping in the same bed. Collected antiques together on New England road trips. Co-hosted cocktail parties for her real estate colleagues.

Going through puberty and adolescence as the cock-teased consort to my mother – confusing and destructive, to say the least – made me even more anxious about sex.

As a teen, I wanted no part of my body. No part of sex. Rejected for overtures to boys my own age, seduced by my own mother, there was no safe place for my sexual desire.

I stopped my fantasies cold. No longer remembered my dreams. No longer knew who I was attracted to, or what I found erotic.

With little privacy, I wanted to come as quickly as possible, jacked off furtively and furiously. No fantasy unspooling in my mind, no object of desire on my bedroom wall. Just me and my own body. That was safe.

For me, early childhood sexual abuse – extended through puberty and adolescence because of my mother – linked terror and pain to pleasure, made me an anxious, sex-avoidant adult. Most children come into their sexuality organically, discover, explore and embrace their sexual selves in the normal course of puberty and adolescence. That was not the case for me.

All I wanted to do was pump the brakes. I even tried to stop my erections. Feeling embarrassed, ashamed and way too vulnerable.

Not wanting libido, not wanting erections – both driven by elevated testosterone – my mind may even have induced my body to lower testosterone during puberty and adolescence, which, I believe, would also have inhibited the growth of my penis.

***

As an adult man trying to have sex with another adult, anxiety (or the terror from unremembered childhood sexual abuse) is not your friend.

Bruce Loeffler

When I came out at twenty-six and started dating gay men in the alien sex-first world of gay bars in the 1970s, I was not comfortable having sex with men I didn't know well. I often found myself on first dates in situations I didn't know how to avoid. As soon as we were in the door, they had their clothes off, so I took mine off too because I was decades away from being self-possessed enough to say, 'Hey, slow down, I need to get to know you before we have sex.' Or even *think* of saying that.

Their raging erections pointed right at me, and I stood there naked and limp, feeling small and mortified. So I asked *them* to fuck *me* to take all the pressure off me and my limp dick. In the gay world, I became a 'bottom' by default, not by choice.

I adopted the same passivity I'd known as a child, but I was anxious and clenched – reflexively, defensively – from unremembered childhood rapes. Disembodied, I didn't even know I *was* clenched. The men who picked me up in gay bars forced their way in, effectively raping me again, while my anal sphincter spasmed painfully, often tearing and bleeding.

Even with long-term partners where I could relax my anus and where I could enjoy 'bottoming,' I still had 'bottom shame.' I couldn't accept that passive 'female' role without feeling diminished as a man.

I also came relatively quickly and got soft right after. Men are supposed to last, to drive their partners wild, to fuck them long enough to make them come. Men are even supposed to stay hard after they come and keep fucking. Men should be able to give their partners multiple orgasms.

Or so I thought.

The idea that I would come too soon was my greatest insecurity and a central reason I hesitated in trying to 'top' another man. It was why I was always anxious and limp in the face of a willing asshole and couldn't fuck another man on demand. I also thought anal intercourse was kind of, well, dirty. Perhaps most of all, unconsciously, I did not want to do to other men what had been done to me as a child and couldn't separate active fucking from rape.

As a further complication, anal intercourse requires a much more emphatic erection than vaginal intercourse. A half-assed boner won't do.

I wanted to fuck other men; I had that energy and was often mis-read as a 'top' in gay bars, but I never pulled it off.

Not once.

That's how diminished my sense of masculine power was as a result of my childhood sexual abuse: I couldn't even fuck.

***

In the gay world of the seventies, the beginning of the gay liberation movement, gay men were trying to overcome the effeminate stereotype of the limp-wristed mincing buffoon that Hollywood had served up in the fifties and sixties. They were trying to assert their masculinity and come out of the shadows. They worked out and beefed up, grew facial hair, dressed butch (think of The Village People singing *YMCA* as a parody). They marched out and proud in the streets.

One thread of the early gay liberation movement was gay men claiming their sexuality, embracing their right to be sexual however they wanted. They extricated sex from its central role in relationships, constructed it as casual, recreational, varied. They reacted against the straight world's stigmatisation of them over rear-entry anal sex: stereotypically always imagined as one man bent over – the 'woman' – taking it up the ass from 'the man' standing behind him.

Gay men in the 70s wanted to be *men*. And they wanted their partners to be *men*, too.

In that world of embracing a hyper-masculinity to compensate for their deep gay male insecurities, a limp penis was anathema, an existential threat. Nothing says masculine like a raging erection and nothing says *not* masculine like impotence.

When I was coming out, there was no patience for my sexual reticence or for my need to get to know my partners before being sexual. I was often rejected for my limp dick and for my inability to 'top' on command. I rarely got to a second date, which only increased my sexual anxiety and shame. I could barely even see myself as a man.

Perhaps my marked anxiety about not being sufficiently masculine coloured my view of my own erection because it was easy to hang my insecurities on the size of my dick. I thought my penis was shorter and smaller than it actually was and I thought I was significantly underhung, which only reinforced my masculine insecurity in an unfortunate negative feedback loop.

***

Penises are a motley lot. They are not the most beautiful part of male anatomy compared to, say, the rounded symmetry and volume of an ass or the planes of a ripped torso. Penises are odd squiggles of flesh, deliberately reduced in size in Greek and Roman and Renaissance sculpture so as not to distract from the beauty of the male body's proportions and muscles. Ever wonder why Michelangelo's *David* was so underhung?

Penises shrink, wrinkle and flop. Hard, they often curve or twist, veering off in one direction or the other. Some erections taper or bulge or have heads significantly smaller or larger than the shaft. And of course, they can have all manner of foreskin or bad circumcisions. But every so often, there's a penis – an erection – whose beauty catches your breath.

I got compliments on the beauty of my penis from my partners. Erect, it has pleasing proportions, is perfectly straight, and I uniform in girth from head to base. It received a careful circumcision (not my choice!) which left a uniform remnant of folded skin. It also has prominent veining. I thought my erection was small, but I also thought my penis was beautiful. *It may not be large, but it's beautiful!* I told myself.

I also had big, bouncy balls, which is seen an additional marker of masculinity, as demonstrated in many common expressions:

'Grow a pair!' means 'man up'.

'That was ballsy!' means something is done with manly bravado and nerve.

'He has some balls!' means someone has overstepped as 'real men' are wont to do.

Like a large cock, large balls imply virility: coursing testosterone, high sperm count, and powerful ejaculations.

I was proud of my large, low-hanging balls. I thought, *If I don't have the meat, at least I have the potatoes!* At least there was some bulge in my briefs. Until the recent decade, that is, when bi-weekly testosterone injections, which are required at seventy-two to keep my testosterone level and libido within range for a man my age, caused my balls to shrink.

But boy, am I a shooter. My gun (or should I say cannon?) might be small, but it sure has fire power, and those powerful ejaculations correlated with five-star orgasms for me. The farther I shot, the more I felt. My penis might not be large, but it's always been a champ for pleasure.

It's amazing the number of ways I tried to reassure myself that I was a powerful, masculine man despite the disempowerment of my early childhood rapes, despite becoming a 'bottom' by default, despite my struggles with impotence and despite thinking I was underhung.

All men, gay or straight, find ways to bolster their sense of masculinity to one degree or another:

- Lift weights. Grow a beard or a moustache. Get a tattoo.
- Choose a 'real man' profession, like soldier, builder, engineer. Drive a big truck, rev an un-muffled muscle car, hug fast curves in a Porsche.
- Take up mixed martial arts. Be a triathlete or Iron Man. Win every fight.
- Strive for a high salary. Accumulate wealth.
- Take up space. Look powerful. Be a man of action.
- Never cry or look weak.
- Shoot a big gun. Swing a big dick.

If you don't (or think you don't) have that – if your sense of yourself as a man was damaged by any means – then compensate, compensate, compensate.

I grew a beard at seventeen. I had a rigid masculine presentation, which is why men who later picked me up in gay bars saw me as a 'top' and expected *me* to fuck *them*. I chose geology to be rugged, to work outdoors, to clamber over rock outcrops wearing Levi's and heavy hiking boots, a rock hammer hanging from my belt. I tore out walls and remodelled houses. Built block walls and patios, planted large trees. I was *buff* from manual labour. I never cried – I couldn't cry or else I'd look weak.

Bruce Loeffler

I used to think that 'size doesn't matter' was just what women learned to say reflexively to reassure notoriously insecure men. I thought it was bullshit. I used to think that size really *did* matter, but I've learned that size is not always what it seems, and really doesn't matter so much, after all, for sex. Sure, some people might have preferences for longer or shorter penises, for cut (circumcised) or uncut, for thinner or fatter. Just like some might have preferences in a woman's breast size. But all kinds of penises get the job done.

Besides, there are many other ways to give pleasure besides fucking. Let's face it: oral sex all by itself is pretty damn hot and it's something 75% of gay men do. Only 40% of gay couples practice anal intercourse, and only half of those reciprocally. In contrast to what most straight people imagine, less than 25% of gay couples organise their sexual lives around anal intercourse, with one man always the 'top' and the other the 'bottom.' That's the beauty of homo sex – everything you can do to someone else, they can also do to you.

Plenty of straight men have discovered the erotic potential of their anuses and prostates by having something up their butts (a finger, a butt plug, a vibrator) to enhance their orgasms. Even so, many of those men keep it a secret out of shame. For other straight men, the mere thought of anal invasion is assault enough on their sense of manhood to make them averse to prostate exams. As my brother-in-law once said, so elegantly, 'It's strictly exit only.'

Some women like anal intercourse, too. The vagina, like the prostate, lies on the other side of the rectal wall and it can be massaged by anal intercourse. The anus and the vagina are part of the web of muscles that make up the pelvic floor, so both vaginal and anal intercourse can stimulate those muscles and can induce rhythmic contractions in the pelvic floor, which enhance orgasms in both men and women.

The body's elimination systems are intimately connected to its sexual systems. Why else is the anus so highly nerve-rich? To make anal fissures and haemorrhoids insanely painful? Or to make the caress of a finger or tongue – or, fully relaxed, the caress of a penis – so sensuous? The anus (as fully washed or douched as you want) can be a dual function organ, used for defecation *and* sex. Just like a penis is a dual function organ used for urination *and* sex.

I understand this now.

People can jump to conclusions – for instance, that my childhood sexual abuse made me gay. But no, I was *born* a gay boy. However, in the 1950s, in a time of strict gender roles and conformity and a time of anti-gay witch hunts, my family couldn't support a gay child. They and society convinced me I was straight. So I had a high school girlfriend, then later married a woman in grad school, and got divorced when I discovered I was gay. My childhood sexual abuse did not *make* me gay, but it did have a heavy impact on how I expressed my adult gay sexuality.

Speaking of jumping to conclusions, my childhood sexual abuse did not make me an abuser as it did my mother and my straight brother, who was also a sex addict and an alcoholic. As a child, my boundaries were obliterated, but as an adult, my boundaries have been firm. I knew how to parent appropriately and was always there, no matter what, for my niece and my nephew and for my college students when they showed up at my door needing support and advice.

***

Bruce Loeffler

It's too bad that so many men, gay and straight, still hang their masculinity on the size of their dicks, on what they like to do in bed, and who they do it with.

Just because you're hung does not mean you're a man.

Just because you're not hung does not make you less of one.

Just because you might be attracted to men does not make you any less of a man. And whether or not you like anal surrender has nothing to do with your manhood.

But I'm sure most men, gay and straight, will go on thinking the opposite of all those things.

What a waste.

I know that it was for me.

The Little Lotus Flower That Could

Aoife E. Osborne

Aoife E. Osborne

When I was nineteen years old, I got my first tattoo. It was during my gap year and it was a charity event. This was not a decision I took lightly, and I do remember having a moment of panic the night before – I felt this immense sense of responsibility, and I started to doubt whether I was making the right decision.

The following day, when it came to the event, so many people turned up – more than anyone had anticipated. The artists quickly realised there wasn't time to tattoo everyone, so I volunteered to get mine another day. When I was suggesting it, it seemed like a good idea. I figured it would give me a few days to think about whether I was really sure, but as soon as the sentence left my mouth, I wanted to take it back. I wanted to jump in a chair and beg the artist to give me my tattoo. It was one of those moments when you make a choice and then instantly realise you've made the wrong one.

A few days later, I was back in the tattoo studio and walked out less than half an hour later with a little lotus flower on the inside of my left angle. The lotus flower typically symbolises rebirth and resilience and in the years prior to the tattoo, I had struggled with depression, anxiety, self-harm, and suicidal ideation. Having finished school and waiting to start university, I chose the lotus flower to represent a new beginning for me and my mental health. Afterwards, when it healed, I found myself gently stroking it at random moments. I found the texture intriguing, and it was oddly satisfying to touch. I wore shorter trousers to show it off and I wore stronger sunscreen to keep it from getting sunburned.

That little tattoo was the start of healing my relationship with my body.

I like to think of it as the first chapter in a new narrative. Fast forward four years to 2022, as I write this little essay about my journey with my body, and I have a grand total of seven tattoos on my arms and legs.

Shortly after the first lotus flower, I had a section of the Sistine Chapel inked on the inside of my right ankle. I chose The Creation of Adam in memory of a twin sibling I lost in the womb. I wanted to find a way to commemorate him and keep him with me. I don't know any of these details about my twin, but in my head, the persona I've created is male and named Adam. I don't think there's any way to fully describe the ongoing grief I have for him, or the survivor's guilt that comes and goes in unpredictable waves, but my tattoo became part of the way to channel it. I think something I had struggled with was the absence of a physical indicator of my twin and getting the tattoo felt like an acknowledgement of his presence, and a way of keeping him with me throughout my life.

Next, I got a pygmy possum on my outer left leg. In school, I'd always been really academic, but Latin was the first subject that I failed miserably. It wasn't for a want of trying; I just happened to be useless at it. When I finally passed after two years of studying, I decided to get a tattoo to commemorate the sense of achievement. In Latin, the verb 'possum' translates to 'I can' or 'I'm able to.' It seemed nice to have such a niche reference, plus I'm a sucker for a bit of wordplay. I even named her Minerva (Minnie, for short) after the Roman goddess of wisdom.

My third tattoo was inspired by Disney Pixar's *Inside Out*. The character Bing Bong wears a multicoloured flower brooch, with each petal representing one of the emotion characters: Joy, Sadness, Anger, Disgust and Fear. After my long history of mental health issues, I wanted to remind myself of the importance of feeling and that all emotions are important. They can exist in harmony, like petals on a flower, and they come together to make something beautiful.

Next, to mirror my pygmy possum, I got an octopus on my right leg after finding a poem called 'The Invisible Octopus' by called Corina Duyn. She wrote the poem based on her battle with myalgic encephalomyelitis (ME), imagining the disorder as an invisible octopus. The poem has the sentence, 'We all have an invisible octopus,' meaning we all have our own internal struggles. My mental illness isn't visible to others, but it's there. I found something poignant and comforting in knowing that everyone has a private battle, and we should be respectful of that. Also, my octopus is named Athena after the Greek goddess of wisdom, to fully complement Minnie the pygmy possum.

Also on the inside of my left leg is a tulip from another charity tattoo event. It was to raise money for autism awareness, which has become hugely important to our family in recent years. My aunt also got a tattoo during the event, and I love the idea that we're linked with our tattoos by something that means so much to us both. I hadn't planned on adding any more tattoos above my lotus, but it just felt like it was meant to be.

Aoife E. Osborne

Weirdly, the artwork was almost identical, even though the tulip artist had never seen my lotus flower. Having one of my most recent tattoos just above my very first tattoo feels cathartic as I see that progression on my body. I liken it to an author releasing a surprise sequel to one of your favourite books: a combination of the nostalgia for the first and excitement for the second.

Finally, my most recent addition is a heart-shaped balloon with the text 'I'm in love' in honour of my favourite series *Crazy Ex-Girlfriend*. If you're not familiar with it, be prepared for a few spoiler alerts.

The main character shares my diagnosis of borderline personality disorder, and this series was monumental in me coming to terms with my diagnosis. The last episode of the series sees the main character realising that before she can love anyone else, she must learn to love herself. This sentiment is something I struggle with every day, but I wanted to keep a piece of the show with me as a reminder of the possibility that someday, I might be capable of fully accepting myself.

When I write these statements and review them, there's a common theme: I wanted them. Each of my tattoos was completely and totally selfish. After a lifetime of being at war with my body, my tattoos have been a way of making peace. Not just with me, but with the outside world too. It goes without saying that with tattoos comes stigma and judgement, along with a slew of unwanted or unprompted questions.

You know that's permanent, right?

Yes, I do. Considering how expensive they are, I actually consider it a bargain.

Are you sure you've thought this through?

Yes, I'm sure. I give each new tattoo careful consideration, I spend hours going over the finest details in the artwork, and I never rush into a new tattoo.

What if you change your mind? You're going to regret that when you're older.

I find this immensely unlikely. The majority of my tattoos have been with me for at least a year, and my fondness for them only grows each day.

What are your kids going to think?

Children who notice them think I'm cool, which is always an instant ego boost. It's something my nerdy teen self could have only dreamt of.

When I'm asked these questions, it's very tempting to reply with a short answer and remind the asker that what I do with my body is none of their business. However, I have been told that this perpetuates the Angry Tattooed Young Woman stereotype.

Instead, I find comfort in reminding myself of this: my tattoos are no one's business but my own. They are, in many ways, the biggest middle finger I can give to wider society. I have them because I want them, and for no other reason. Despite the theme of self-love which runs through them, the very act of choosing tattoos is the greatest act of self-love and self-assurance I've ever given myself. They are a constant reassurance simply by being a constant. Whatever changes come my way in the future, my tattoos will always be a part of me. They will age with me. They will remind me of the challenges I've overcome and the progress I've made. They allow me to express myself unapologetically.

I'm sure people do think something, and when they do, I hope my tattoos give them an interesting internal dialogue. I'd like to emphasise that I don't care, but I do wonder with an amused curiosity. Sometimes, I wonder what they think my tattoos mean, and despite myself, I like to imagine the stories they associate with them. I wonder if I anger them, if they think I'm corrupting society, if they think I'm the definition of what's wrong with the world today or if I'm a bad influence on future generations.

Ironically, despite a general consensus that they may find my tattoos off-putting or inappropriate, children are far more accepting of tattoos than most grown-ups are. Usually, they find the bright colours exciting and the artwork interesting, and then they move on. Sometimes, they barely notice them at all. Children are, in my experience, inherently more forgiving and accepting, and the judgements they impose are frequently influenced by their parents. In terms of my own future children (should I be so lucky), I like to think my tattoos will teach them to celebrate their bodies and spare them the years of shame that I suffered.

When children are taught to worry about what other people think of their choices, they learn that our bodies are the property of everyone else and subject to their judgements. They learn to be aware of their weight, their hair, the colour of their skin, and how they dress. When they learn that tattoos are rebellious, that pink hair is unacceptable or that they need to dress a certain way to avoid staring, they lose the ability to express themselves. They will follow fashion trends and obey what the diet industry tells them and be governed by the preferences of a classist, sexist system that would rather people conform until everyone is a faceless copy.

If they are lucky, they will find an ounce of rebellion in themselves and use it to buy a tub of semi-permanent hair dye, a pair of ripped jeans and a lotus tattoo on their inner left ankle. If they are really lucky, this will happen sooner rather than later.

The art of self-expression and self-love should not be an act of rebellion. It should not need to be selfish. It should just be. I'm not saying I think everyone should get a tattoo or dye their hair some random colour of the rainbow, because contrary to what romantic comedies will tell you, I don't think a dramatic makeover is always the answer. What I do wonder is what everyone would do if the population no longer cared what others thought of them. How many people would change their wardrobe, get that tattoo, eat a decent meal, and forget about the diet that a social media advert sold them? How many people would stop holding their bodies hostage to the expectations of other people, and instead find new ways to celebrate them?

I read somewhere once that our bodies are our temples, and our tattoos are stained glass windows. I've never really agreed with this statement, mostly because I struggle to think of my body as a temple. To me, temples are places of worship, grandeur, faith, and belief, none of which are adjectives I equate with my body. Even after years of body positivity becoming a mainstream topic, I still struggle with the idea of loving my body. To be frank, I don't. To me, it's a vessel. It brings me from one point to another, but it's not perfect.

It's too short, and this causes several daily inconveniences. Some would say it's too fat, and it makes me self-conscious. Every few months, my polycystic ovaries decide to throw a fit and they cause debilitating pain. My baby teeth were enamel deficient and had to be removed when I was six. My nails are brittle and refuse to grow. My arms have patches of discoloration from episodes of self-harm in my teenage years. My eyes need glasses to see properly. My back aches and cracks on a daily basis. My body is not my temple. It is a vessel that gets me through my day, from A to B, and sometimes it doesn't even do that.

I am a writer and a reader. Putting those together means that I am a lover of stories. I prefer to think of my body as a story and my tattoos as the accompanying illustrations. They're an acknowledgement of the triumphs I've had, of all the days I have successfully managed to be a person and all the future days I hope to enjoy. They are tangible proof that somehow, I have held on longer than my suicidal seventeen-year-old self could ever have imagined. They are with me every minute of every day, like my own little private cheerleading team.

When I shower, when I get dressed, when I cook, clean, wash my hands – when I type silly little essays on my silly little computer, and I catch a glimpse of the pink balloon on my wrist, I am reminded of my promise to myself to survive.

I am reminded, every day, several times a day, that I am strong.

I am not alone.

I am smart, but I'm also still learning.

I am resilient.

I am loved.

I am broken and cracked and imperfect and that's ok because I am me.

I am a survivor, and I deserve to celebrate my survival every day.

From my first little lotus flower to my new heart balloon, my tattoos are a part of the story that I am learning to tell.

My Journey to Full Exposure

Iris Leona Marie Cross

Iris Leona Marie Cross

I concealed it for most of my life, not daring to expose it. No amount of exercise or dieting could reduce it to an acceptable size. I was stuck with the behemoth for life and obsessed with hiding it. Then came March 2020, a life changer. Ironically, with its restrictions – wear masks, wash hands, watch your distance – Covid-19 was an unexpected liberator for me.

Some women defied L'Oréal's vintage hair dye advertisement ('Don't Grow Old Graysfully. Fight It Every Step of The Way') by growing grey and *not* fighting it every step of the way. Stay-at-home work-from-home mandates released women from the bondage of dyeing their grey hair. No more covering up their natural hair colour to hide their age, spending unnecessary money at the hair salon, wasting time at home disguising their grey roots themselves, and adhering to society's youth-obsessed norms. Women took to social media to talk about embracing their grey hair. They told Vogue, Time, InStyle, The New Yorker, and The New York Times, to name a few, how liberating it was to ditch the dye.

'With grey hair, I actually feel powerful,' one woman admitted.

Iris Leona Marie Cross

'Going grey in the pandemic made me feel younger,' said another. Why hadn't they freed themselves from these shackles long before? This was the question they asked.

I asked myself the same question. My musings, however, had nothing to do with hair colour. My genetics were kind to me in this respect but merciless in another: namely, my huge forehead. Growing up, the only other person I knew with an oversize forehead was the neighbour's niece, one of the top models in the country. I admired her height, the trendy clothes she wore, and how she carried herself: elegance personified. She stood out, and so did her forehead. Pity, I thought. She would have been far prettier were it not for that forehead. People said the same about America's Next Top Model host, Tyra Banks. 'When I turned into a supermodel, a lot of people were saying, "She cute, but she got a big forehead."'

Like Tyra's critics, I have never been fond of large foreheads, including my own, although how my perceptions and hang-ups about forehead size emerged is unknown. Somewhere along my life's journey, I received the message loud and clear that large foreheads should be covered up.

As a child, Popeye the Sailor was a favourite cartoon of mine, along with the Flintstones. Wilma Flintstone and Betty Rubble, Wilma's neighbour, were pretty. Popeye's long-time love interest, Olive Oyl, was ugly. A feisty character, Olive Oyl always tied her black hair back in a bun, exposing her large forehead. Maybe these cartoons helped to shape my views since I don't recall anyone telling me or even implying that a large forehead was unattractive. No one called me ugly or 'five-head' as Tyra Banks experienced. Perhaps it's because, from a very early age, my mother gave me centre parts and side parts that covered up chunks of the forehead. She never brushed my hair back. If this was intentional, I am grateful to her for protecting me from playground bullies.

From that time to pre-Covid-19, my forehead remained concealed. Bandanas, caps, berets, headscarves, bangs, fringes, curls, side parts, and center parts did a great job. Any attempt to remove them was met with hostility. Although I wished I could tie my hair back, that option scared me stiff.

One evening, I had a function to attend and wondered if I should free my forehead for the night. I sought advice from a young ten-year-old stylist because children would be truthful.

'How should I wear my hair? This way… or that way?'

'Uhm… uhm… can you show me again?'

'This way, with hair on my face, or that way with hair pulled back?'

'Uhm…'

'Well, which way? Make up your mind.'

'I think the first way looks better.'

A crushing blow. No chance I'd risk wearing my hair pulled back, given that damning verdict. I never asked her why the covered-up forehead hairstyle looked better. I couldn't bear to hear the answer, and I didn't want to put her on the spot. I knew she wouldn't want to hurt my feelings. So, the cover-up continued.

Years on, standing in front of the changing room mirror at the gym, combing my wet hair, I heard, 'OMG! Why don't you wear your hair like that?'

Being caught with my pants down couldn't have been more embarrassing. In a panic, I reached for my knitted woollen cap, pulling it as far down my forehead as possible. The voice belonged to my colleague who had accompanied me to the gym.

I thought it was safe to expose my forehead because I saw no one around.

'Why don't you leave your hair like that? You look lovely with it pulled back,' she repeated.

'No, I don't!'

'You do.'

'Yuck. It's unattractive.'

'Are you crazy?'

'Please, let's not talk about it,' I said, feeling uncomfortable about her seeing me so exposed. Her enthusiasm for my forehead didn't matter. I continued the cover-up.

In August 2020, the mother of one of my close friends died, and they asked me to do a reading at her funeral. Masks were mandatory and attendance was limited to five. How was I to connect with online mourners wearing a mask, hair cascading down my forehead, and my tiny eyes barely visible? I considered combing my hair back for the occasion. Did I dare? Many dress rehearsals later, with trepidation, I bared my forehead for the first time.

'Your sister and I thought you looked good,' my brother-in-law messaged after viewing the funeral online from their home overseas. He was familiar with my lifelong forehead insecurity, frequently hammering home the scientific view that large foreheads are associated with intelligence.

'Intelligence, maybe. Attractiveness? Never! Not in my opinion.'

He disagreed. Besides, look at the number of attractive movie stars and singers throughout history who had big foreheads, he argued. But neither he nor anyone else could make me see beauty in an oversize forehead.

Still, after the funeral, I felt tempted to test the waters on a larger scale by walking the streets with my forehead exposed. This was the ultimate test because I lived in the street harassment capital of the world. Daily, women received unsolicited comments about every aspect of their anatomy. Once, while standing in line at the post office, the customer behind me touched my shoulder. I turned around. He said I was lucky he wasn't Count Dracula because Dracula's fangs would have pierced my succulent neck as I queued.

I planned to debut my forehead in this inviting environment where no body part – necks or foreheads – was off-limits to street harassers. After all, fortune favoured the brave.

The day had come. Anxious, I stood in front of the bathroom mirror, wondering if I had the backbone to do as planned. I pulled my hair back in a top bun, attached my mask, donned a pair of sunglasses, breathed in two lungs full of courage, and began the walk from home to the market twenty minutes away.

My heart pounded against my chest, and my breathing got shallower and shallower with each step I took. I felt like everybody was watching me and thinking, 'Gosh, what an enormous forehead!' I refused to lock eyes with passersby, including those who said good morning. People were so polite that day. What a surprise! Things were looking up, even though my eyes looked down to avoid eye contact.

As I approached the market entrance, the guard held his hand up. No more shoppers were allowed in as per Covid-19 restrictions. Then he changed his mind.

'Beautiful lady, I'll let you alone in.'

Beautiful? I said to myself. *Did he see my forehead?* The response to my exposed forehead was heartening. I received affirmations instead of condemnations. I was never so appreciative of feedback from street harassers. The outing was a turning point.

Almost two years since the historic day I exposed my forehead to public scrutiny, I still struggle to embrace this part of my body. Forehead-endowed celebrities like Angelina Jolie, Rihanna, Tyra Banks, Caroline Wozniacki, Reese Witherspoon, and Zoe Saldana have no qualms displaying their large foreheads with pride and pizzazz. I haven't yet reached that level of comfort, and maybe I never will. I continue to seek security in a dangling tendril or a few slicked-down edges framing my face. When I can walk the streets with my hair pulled back, my forehead in full view, and not feel naked, uneasy, or vulnerable, I'll know I am healed from my forehead dysmorphia.

One thing's for sure: I won't resort to cosmetic surgery, and its associated risks, as one woman has done. Interviewed in Huda Beauty, she confessed to always having an issue with her forehead. 'For as long as I can remember, I have hated how large my forehead was. My hair was always styled with a side fringe, I would never face the direction of the wind in case it exposed my forehead, and I hated that I felt I could never just scrape my hair back off my face.'

So, she arranged an $8,000 USD foreheadplasty, flying from her home in the US to a clinic in London, England. Her operation was a huge success and she had no regrets. Other forehead dysmorphics flooded the online magazine's comments section asking for updates and help in finding surgeons where they lived who were skilled at performing forehead reductions.

'Hello, do you have a clinic in Turkey?'

'I wonder if the doc has any recommendations for doctors in Denver.'

'I love how the shorter forehead made her cheeks look fuller. *So* pretty.'

'My forehead is an airport, my God.'

'I am so glad this is possible.'

'I want to do this as well because my forehead is huge.'

There's a limit to my bravery, which only extends to walking the streets with my forehead fully exposed in the full glare of a critical public.

As Popeye the Sailor Man often said, 'I yam what I yam and that's all what I yam.' The road to self-acceptance is long, and I'm taking it one step at a time.

Does Anything Taste as Good as Skinny Feels?

Bex Thorp

Bex Thorp

Over the years, body image has been discussed over and over again, even as the idea of what the 'perfect' body type is changes. There are constant public discussions about what we should look like and how we should always be dissatisfied with our bodies. We're told we should always be on some kind of improvement journey to make ourselves slimmer, fitter, healthier – something other than what we already are. It's ridiculous that we are forced to scrutinise ourselves on a daily basis.

I have disliked my body and been unhappy with my image for as long as I can remember. When I was young, I always felt like the chubby friend, the one who stood by and watched her slimmer, prettier, more confident friends get the attention. I was the happy, bubbly girl but never felt like the thin, pretty one. When I look back at the pictures now, I realise that was absolutely ridiculous. I was a gorgeous healthy-looking teenager and I had no reason to feel that way, except that society constantly told me I had to be a UK size six in order to be happy.

As I grew up, my attitude to health and weight stayed the same. I cannot remember a time when I was not on some form of diet. Throughout university, I cut out massive food groups, tried milkshake diets (they didn't last long), noodle diets, points-based diets, and protein-only based diets (that one was particularly unenjoyable). I went to parties and tried to drink vodka and water rather than Coke because it fit with the plan, even though I absolutely hate vodka.

I calorie counted until it became obsessive. My husband would make dinner and ask me if I was 'allowed' to have certain things as part of my diet. How wrong is that question? It is absolutely laughable when I think back to those days. I spent so much of my life demonising food and drinks and labelling foods as 'bad' and 'good' that I lost sight of how to enjoy food and just be me.

I can't even begin to imagine how much money I must have spent over the years on various diet products, lifestyle plans, health groups, and fool proof exercise equipment that began to gather dust as soon as I bought it. Now I can think of so many better uses for that money. I have been sucked into every diet system, every one of which promised the world and said they could make dreams come true. They said they could help me achieve my better self, but who were they to decide who that self should be? Why does a 'better self' have to be slim, toned, and fit? Why does it have to be a size ten or smaller to be accepted?

It has taken me a long time to come to this realisation and begin to make peace with my body, but I have wasted so many years of my life chasing the idea that 'nothing tastes as good as skinny feels'. The person who coined that phrase[3] certainly wasn't someone who was thinking about mental health.

Diet culture is so toxic and has done untold damage to so many people – it has led to eating disorders and diets that are just unmanageable. I'm finally at the point where I can try to fix my relationship with food. Don't get me wrong, I still revert to the old adage of, 'Oh I shouldn't have that cake, it's bad for me' or 'Today is my cheat day', but I'm working hard to change.

Recently, the conversation around diet culture and body image has begun to change. There are more dieticians and nutritionists who are sharing their thoughts on how diets and the harm and it is beginning to emerge that diets are not actually good for you. There is a shift towards intuitive eating, which involves listening to your body and your fullness cues. Essentially, this means returning to eating as we did when we were children. We knew how to eat before diet culture wormed its way into our consciousness. We ate when we were hungry and stopped when we were full.

I can't remember the last time I did that. Studies have proven that while we may lose weight with different diet plans, this weight rarely stays off long term. In fact, more often than not, people actually put all the weight back on and then some. This is because these diet plans are not sustainable. They may restrict whole food groups, force you to choose one food group over another, or ask you to count calories and log every item of food you consume. All these things are unachievable long term. Our bodies are clever. They realise that we are not

---

[3] Supermodel Kate Moss

being fuelled correctly and begin to revolt. Then the yo-yo dieting starts again and we're stuck in a cycle of losing weight, putting it back on, starting a new diet, losing more weight, and then putting it all back on again. It's a miserable cycle.

Now, while I am becoming a strong advocate of ditching the diet and being happy in my own body, this does not mean I'm going to start stuffing my face with cakes, doughnuts, chocolate, and burgers, and damn the consequences. I am also realistic: I know that there are health risks to being overweight, including high blood pressure, heart disease, diabetes, strokes, and liver disease. I know, that because I carry more weight around my stomach, I have a higher risk of suffering from one or more of these health issues. That does not sit well with me either. I think we have to understand the risks and how we can combat these without subjecting ourselves to rigorous, unachievable diet plans that make us feel miserable. I will still try to lose a few pounds around my middle, but I want to find a way to do this well and have long-term results.

The word diet comes from the Greek word dietata, which means 'way of life'. A diet should not be a restrictive way of eating, but a whole way of life. It should be an enjoyable experience, fuelling our bodies to get the best out of them, but also be sustainable. I am a huge believer in food having a purpose. It should be enjoyed with friends and family – shared, experienced, and valued.

At the risk of sounding like a cliché, all food is good food as long as it is eaten in moderation. No food should have a higher value than any other, and no one should be judged for the food choices they make. Of course there are foods that are more nutritious and serve our bodies more than others by filling us with energy and vitality, but they can also be enjoyed along with the less nutritious choices.

I used to constantly chase the idea that slimmer is better, that skinny was healthy, and that I would be a better person if I lost three stone. Since having my son, though, I have not shrunk back to my super slim size eight/ten body. I tried to get there at the beginning, but with a baby attached to my hip, I couldn't find the time or the energy to do my body pump and high cardio classes four times a week. I was exhausted and needed high energy foods and snacks. I gave up trying to fit into my pre-pregnancy clothes and instead gave them all away to charity a few months ago.

I realise that my body has changed. It created, nurtured, and birthed a beautiful boy. It is an amazing vessel and I am thankful to it for allowing me to do that. Would I like to have a bit less fat around my stomach, no bingo wings, and a smaller bum? Yes, but I would prefer to be able to run around after my son and play energetic games with him. I would prefer to be able to touch my toes without feeling like my insides are being squashed into oblivion. I would prefer to improve my sleep quality and stop waking my husband up with my snoring! I would prefer to climb two flights of stairs at home without being out of breath at the top. All these things are long-term goals that require a lifestyle change, not a short-term diet fix. It will be a slower journey, but the benefits will be worth it.

I am determined, like many others, to say no to diet culture and am going to attempt to feel gratitude for my body and for all the things it allows me to do. It is strong, it holds me up, it moves me from place to place, and it enables me to spend time with my family and friends. It is magnificent and I need to be more aware of that! There will be days when I don't feel this positivity and days when I don't like what I see in the mirror, but I hope those will become fewer. I hope that I can retrain my brain to look for the good in my body, to nourish it and fuel it well and to give it what it needs to function and move in a fun and enjoyable way. I am a work in progress, but it is work I am happy to undertake.

I have come a long way since my younger days. I wish I could go back and tell myself to stop worrying about my weight, to throw away the scales and focus on the more important things in life. I have had a great, enjoyable, and happy life, but sometimes I wonder what more could have been enjoyed had I not spent my time comparing myself to others and wishing I looked different.

Hairy Legs

Premalatha Karupiah

Premalatha Karupiah

I hardly ever wore a short skirt or dress. I was mostly in a *salwar kameez,* a pair of pants and a top, or a sari. Every now and then, long dresses and skirts. All of these would cover my legs because I was not comfortable wearing a short skirt or dress that showed my legs.

While growing up, I don't remember my mom or siblings talking to me about shaving or waxing my legs, though of course we talked about all the physical changes I would experience growing up. I used to think that I grew up in a somewhat traditional family, so such conversations would come under the purview of my mom. However, unlike most traditional families, I had amazing conversations with my dad about many topics. I didn't even know that dads don't usually cook until my classmates acted surprised when I told them my dad cooked for us. In the later part of my life, I realised that my family was far more progressive than I thought.

Coming from a family that did not teach or impose beauty norms, it was a rude shock when I was criticised, many times, for wearing a short skirt with my hairy legs and constantly told that I must shave or wax them.

'Women's legs should be smooth,' they said.

'Hairy legs are ugly,' another said.

Some even implied that I am not a hygienic person because I don't shave.

'What else don't you shave?' they asked.

It didn't even occur to me until my late teens that women were expected to have smooth legs and no body hair. People also commented on my hairy hands, which was a worse shock than the hairy legs comments, but hairy hands have never bothered me. I have never even entertained the idea of removing that hair and I have never covered them. My only solace in all this was I never heard such criticism from my own family.

On the rare occasions when I wore a short dress, I would wear it with pantyhose, only to be told that the colour of my pantyhose was too light for my dark skin, which made it look ridiculous. Other times, I was laughed at for being old-fashioned because pantyhose is an outdated accessory and did not look natural on me.

The idea that looking natural is part of being beautiful is one oxymoron I have failed to understand. Every time someone talks about stereotypical beauty standards and looking natural in the same sentence, it irks me – there is nothing 'natural' about beauty standards. Beauty standards come with an expectation that women's bodies are only beautiful when modified, either by using make-up or other techniques, invasive and non-invasive alike.

What does 'natural' make-up even mean? How can one be natural if they are wearing make-up and how is it natural for women to shave their legs? I know many women who enjoy make-up and are happy to shave or wax their legs and practice many types of beauty practices. I respect that. I didn't become a feminist to tell women what to do but because I believe women should make choices that are comfortable and meaningful to them. But when a notion of beauty is constantly shoved down my throat in everyday life as well as in movies, media, and in schools, it makes me want to throw up.

Due to the constant criticisms, I tried waxing once and then vowed I would never do it again. Somehow, though, I couldn't bring myself to show my hairy legs, so I just wore clothes that covered my legs. I guess those criticisms affected me more than I realised.

The strange thing is that I was generally very confident about my physical appearance. As a teenage girl, I was seen as boring and, to some extent, ugly because I never bothered to style myself. Other than cutting my hair to look even, I have never styled my hair and have used make-up maybe less than five times in my life. I was never good at using make-up and did not like myself on the extremely rare occasions when I succumbed to the pressure and put it on.

On the occasions when I don't conform to stereotypical beauty standards, my attitude has always been, 'If you don't like me, look away!'

Sometimes I say it out loud to all the 'well-meaning' people who criticise me, but other times I say it in my head, especially when dealing with older people. In my culture, talking back to elders is extremely frowned upon.

It still perplexes me that I didn't use that same attitude with the people who criticised my legs. I guess somewhere along the way, I must have internalised the idea that women should not have hairy legs. Have you ever seen a beautiful woman with hairy legs in a movie or an ad? Even advertisements for women's shavers show women shaving already bare legs because hairy legs are such a taboo, you can't even see them in an ad. As much as I resisted stereotypical beauty standards, this was hard to reject.

It took me many years to resist this 'hairy legs' pressure but now, I am able to step out of my house in a short skirt. No pantyhose: just my bare legs with all the hair. I did get a few stares, but I guess now that I am older, people have given up on me and moved on to gossip and make other young women's lives miserable. It took me a while to get here, but I am finally in a place where I am just happy with myself and my body.

And my attitude towards anyone who thinks my legs are ugly?

'If you don't like it, look away!'

Wardrobe Wednesdays

Matt McGee

Matt McGee

All I had to do to change my body image was go to a garage sale.

My father was a regular of our city's garage sale circuit. I couldn't remember the last time he'd bought anything new – shoes, tires, clothes, books, anything. When he passed away four years ago, he owned six sets of used golf clubs. Dad wasn't a hoarder. He just loved a bargain and had plenty of garage space.

I, on the other hand, lived a minimal life and would run something into the ground – shoes, clothes, cars, so on. Then I'd drop into a mall with the tread flapping on my Sketchers or ratty T-shirt bearing the logo of a band that had broken up ten years earlier. Forget collector's item status: the shirt's shoulders, collar and main panel had finally lost all its fights with the washing machine.

But at least I bought new. Always.

Then last year I was driving across town, just minding my own business, when mounted to a telephone pole hung a handmade cardboard sign: GARAGE SALE. An arrow pointed into the neighbourhood. Helpless against my own genetics, I hung my head, turned the wheel, and followed.

For the better part of the last year, I've justified this genetic inevitability by filling my need for books. I go through a new book every two days, so replenishing my supply has been my gateway excuse.

'Got any books?' I'll ask as I climb another driveway. A finger will point and I'll dig out a dusty old Zane Grey or other long-forgotten title from a trunk. Once I've wrangled up what the seller has to offer, it seems only polite to browse whatever else is lying around. Housewares, old tools – and clothes, always clothes.

It wasn't until summer kicked in and I realised all I had for shorts was a ten-year-old pair of grey Quicksilver surf baggies that I opened my mind. I'd just bagged a 100-year-old book on backyard beekeeping for a dollar when I noticed the long table of gently used clothing. I stopped. I looked. Then I pointed.

'How much for the shorts?'

The next morning, having washed my new shorts thoroughly and dried them in the summer sun, I pulled them on and zipped them up. A little snug but they held true. I reached in my closet for a blue T-shirt bought on a trip to Colorado the year before; I'd run out of clean clothes and this tee with the state logo was all the corner gas station in Boulder had available. It was a medium.

I pulled it on and felt it slide over my torso. Ninety percent of everything I own has the right logo for whatever mood I wake up in, but they're mostly in XL or XXL. Don't even get me started about the baggy gangsta styles of the early 2000s and the dick tent effect.

Matt McGee

I grabbed my car keys and drove across town to my favourite sports bar, where the salads are good and the drinks are cold. I headed for a table where NASCAR was on when my favourite server spotted me.

'Hey, lookin' sharp!'

I looked at her with a scrunched brow.

'Really! Did you lose weight?'

I looked down. 'You like it? Shorts are from a garage sale.' Then I tugged on the T-shirt. 'This came from a 7-11 in Boulder.'

She nodded, I think in part to hide her desire to say, *why can men do this and look right?* 'Well, you look good, like you've slimmed down.'

After a few cold drinks, it was time to hit the men's room, where there's a full-length mirror most of us ignore. This day, though, I stopped and looked.

She was right. Between the size 34 shorts (I'd been swimming in a pair of baggy 38s that create a bad case of chicken legs) and the blue gas station shirt, I looked twenty pounds lighter. The shorter sleeves highlighted the toned nature of my arms. The shorts showed that my legs were actually carved. I didn't look the way I imagined. I looked... slim.

I walked out of the restroom a little straighter, with a little more confidence in my step.

***

Like a lot of people, I'd been suffering from low body image. For many of us, the idea we have of how we look, sometimes based on how we feel that particular day, is often skewed to the point of feeling fatter, dumpier, or more unworthy than we actually are. We carry this around like a backpack full of rocks that slouch our shoulders and slow our gait.

A more severe form is called body dysmorphia, an actual mental health condition in which a person will fixate on a single flaw or perceived flaw and obsessively try to correct it. Compliments don't help; body dysmorphics don't hear them, they just fixate harder.

My version was a bit less than that. What I'd arrived at over a period of years was more of an image degradation. Over time, my wardrobe and lack of will to look at myself in a mirror shifted me away from the hyperawareness I'd taken away from my college years. It became less and less important to me through my thirties and forties. The message on the shirt, or its history, was more important than how it looked on me.

Meanwhile, I'd remained physically active. I play goalie in local hockey leagues three days a week and work seven nights at a job that requires hours of physical movement. My body has to keep moving, so I feed it well. If I don't, it breaks down. I can't afford to be sidelined and no one likes a goalie that can't show.

For our recent family reunion, I was nominated Activities Director; for my second lieutenant, I chose a cousin who's still active in soccer and softball leagues. I didn't realise it, but we're kind of the family jocks.

Yet until I was nominated, I never knew this is how the family saw me. Maybe it was inevitable and I was just the last to acknowledge it. In previous years I'd been the one criss-crossing the picnic site, rallying up players, putting gloves or a bat in their hands, even assigning a volleyball-playing cousin in a leg brace to be umpire. But an organiser?

I guess I was, and everyone saw it. The only one out of the know was me.

***

Matt McGee

One of my favourite clothing items has been in rotation since the mid-2000s. I bought the Levi's straight off the shelf in JC Penny's, or wherever jeans were being sold back in the Bush era.

They went everywhere I went for a while, and then, like the way of all jeans, once the knees and seat started blowing out, it was time for new ones. But instead of falling to the bottom of the rotation, something else happened: I learned how to sew.

Every hockey player has a pair of hockey jeans – denim so torn and shredded that we look like castoffs from Wayne's World. As a pair wore out, I'd toss them in a corner of the closet and eventually decide which ones deserved saving and cut pieces from another 'donor pair.' What I ended up with were the perfect hockey pants, or what I started to call Frankenjeans.

My hockey pants and I became a statement of 'I'll be on the rink later today' or 'I just came from a game.' And since I'd invested hours behind a sewing machine, repairing what most would argue isn't worth the labour, the pants became a statement: I'm a survivor, just like my pants.

I didn't wear them every day – just when a hockey jersey would be hiding my upper body. If I wore an LA Kings jersey, it was practically an advertisement that there was a game on that night. This Kevin Smith-esque fashion move, a colourful guy muumuu, also covers a lot of ground: it shows a support for your city, your team, and implies you can still play a sport. Best of all, those big jerseys hide a lot of perceived flaws.

But the Frankenjeans were louder than it all.

I didn't always top them off with something so bulky. I had a wardrobe of T-shirts bearing a message for every occasion, but they were stretching, fading, tearing, and had been bought in sizes too large for my actual weight and body type – a body type that didn't match the image in my mind.

On a certain level, the shirts matched the pants, but regardless of their individual message, I was sending a larger, more comprehensive one: I'm fading, falling out of fashion, and am secretly hoping others don't see it.

My image degradation might have gone overlooked by my circle of friends. They were used to seeing me in these things. They'd seen all the top guns in my arsenal. I imagined that seeing me in it brought them a certain comfort. It got so that all I had to do was buy a new tee from a secondhand store, and sure enough, I'd get positive comments.

Then it occurred to me: I don't even have to do much to succeed at this.

That's when Wardrobe Wednesday kicked in.

***

I set a reminder on my phone that coincided with my wake-up call: WARDROBE WEDNESDAY would remind me that, before I did anything else on Hump Day, I'd hit up a Goodwill or other store of my choice. I didn't have to spend much, but replacing what had long ago worn out was priority number one.

The first thing that needed replacing were my shoes. I visited DSW with a couple hundred in cash and both pairs went, as did my recent need for Advil. I considered holding a late-night, proper burial to the nineties high-tops, but just deposited them into a neighbour's garbage bin and sent off the 'newer' pair (2014) in a Goodwill donation bin. My foot pain was gone in seventy-two hours.

The following Wednesday, a friend was having a surprise party. As he's a big fan of dress shirts bearing lite beer cans or ears of corn, I honoured his special day with a collared button-up from a Salvation Army store, its material a pattern of little Dutch boys like the image found on paint cans. I wore it twice and donated it back to the same store.

The garage sales became the lifeblood, though. The shorts and odd vintage finds, washed up and made new. And I kept playing hockey. The definition of my forearms continued, as did my general overall health.

Pretty soon I was piling up donations. A few months into Wardrobe Wednesdays, I was browsing a rack of tees in the local thrift store and spotted a familiar image: it was one of my old concert tees.

I didn't buy it, despite what they say about loving something and setting it free.

Meanwhile, the torn, shredded Frankenjeans marched on. That is, until it changed the way most things do: with a snide remark from someone much, much younger.

I'd just walked out of the grocery store where the pants had collected another 'Whoa!' comment from the cashier. I passed a cluster of outdoor tables where a half dozen teenagers were hanging. At the sight of a man their father's age striding along in shaggy they-were-once-pants pants, a silence fell over the table. Eyes dipped down at iPhones.

When I was supposedly out of hearing range, a boy's voice said, 'Whoa, someone call Triple-A because there's been a blowout.'

I had to give him credit for cleverness, but the schoolyard laughter that followed was something I thought I'd left behind lifetimes ago. Yet it still happens and just when you think you've outgrown its ability to cut, there you are, bleeding all over a grocery store parking lot again.

Matt McGee

Snide laughter somehow retains its ability to wilt your insides the way it wilted you back then. We always have an innate desire to be accepted and a fear of being devoured by the pack. So why hadn't I felt that way with my contemporaries? Maybe around them, the Frankenjeans had felt like a trophy. Either way, I decided this was their last day. I drove home, ready to change out of them for the last time.

It had been the armpit of summer and I'd been sweating. The Mets shirt I'd chosen had served its purpose: I'd watched the game, they'd lost, and it was ok to strip it off and throw the shirt in the hamper.

I chose a plain Chardonnay tee off a hanger that, when pulled on, hugged my sides. It had no label inside the neck so the only way to know it was on the right way was to check the left seam where extra tags are often placed. I pulled it on, turned toward the full-length mirror and pulled up the left hem.

When I lifted the shirt, I saw something else: the side I exposed wasn't fat and doughy like it had been years ago. It also wasn't like the chub-laden waistlines of teammates my age I'd see in the locker room.

Instead, my side was lean. There was a good slope to it, with just the right amount of exposed ribs. The tag was there, but so was a body that, frankly, I'd neglected to look at very often. I wasn't the owner of a mid-life train wreck, derailed by a high-carb diet. This looked ok. I pulled my shirt back down and left the pants on.

The sun had just dipped below the ridgeline. I need to wear glasses after sundown to drive. It's just the way my eyes are now.

Did I mention my glasses are six years old? They're not even mine; an ex-girlfriend left them on the nightstand and,

Matt McGee

when I slid them on out of goofiness, I found I could miraculously see better in the dark. I inherited the gift of night vision when she left them behind in the morning.

Now, the lenses are cracked and the frames are missing an earpiece. It's the left one, so whenever someone rides with me, they're sitting on the passenger side and don't really notice. No one's noticed the cracked lens, either. Maybe they just figure that, considering the pants, it's part of the ensemble.

I took out my cell and opened the calendar. Still three more days until Wardrobe Wednesday. I edited the entry with the note: OPTOMETRIST.

I'll probably keep the ex's pair as a backup. Or maybe after I get my new ones, I'll drop over and leave them in her mailbox. She'll likely never know how they were a perfect metaphor for my refreshed wardrobe, or for that matter, our relationship: some things you just outgrow.

Social Justice is Key to Eating Disorder Recovery

Sarah Wirth

Sarah Wirth

If you had told me when I first started university that my studies in social science would be key to my eating disorder recovery, I would have been very confused. At the time, I saw my issues around food and my body as deeply personal problems that were located within myself, perhaps caused by my genetics or my disposition. I had no idea that these experiences were actually tied into a complex web of social systems like diet culture and fatphobia, which influence how we see and value our own bodies and the bodies of others.

    I have had a turbulent relationship with food since I was young, but my struggles with eating issues really amplified when I hit puberty. At the time, I wasn't cognisant of why, but now I can see that it was probably caused, at least in part, by my unquestioned exposure to fatphobia and diet culture, as well as being deeply in denial about my queerness. Together, these experiences left me feeling alienated from myself and very uncomfortable in my body and appearance.

    Like many people, I was exposed to a lot of unconscious weight stigma and fatphobia while growing up. It was everywhere, from family members openly criticised about their body's appearance to food policing and restricted access to 'bad' foods to no one questioning when I ran every morning despite having shin splints. This exposure to diet culture led to my own deeply-embedded and internalised fatphobia and the idea that my body was wrong and needed to change by any means necessary.

At this time, I was also desperately trying to deny the fact that I was queer. I used my eating disorder to try and ignore this part of my identity and suppress my feelings of fear and isolation. These behaviours were also a way for me to try and change the parts of my body which were making me increasingly uncomfortable as they became more obviously female, such as my growing boobs, hips, and thighs. Much later in life, I was finally able to understand this connection between my eating disorder, my sexuality, and my gender identity.

My eating disorder continued to worsen during high school and into university. While my behaviours were becoming increasingly severe, the unquestioned diet culture I was surrounded by meant that my excessive food restriction, overexercising, binge eating, and obsession with my weight and shape was so normalised that it was not until I started purging through vomiting that I was even able to recognise that something might be wrong.

My spiral into my eating disorder eventually landed me in a psychologist's chair. Despite only agreeing to seek treatment in the hope of reducing my binge-eating episodes so I could stop 'self-sabotaging' my weight loss attempts, there was also a small part of me that really hoped that treatment might help me recover.

Sadly, this could not have been further from what happened. During treatment, the psychologist projected a lot of her own fatphobia onto me, which in turn exacerbated my own fear of weight gain and losing control over my body. Rather than helping me to understand and address my internalised fatphobia, poor body image, or the underlying emotional reasons for my behaviours, the psychologist suggested that I could resolve my binging through further restriction. For example, one of her solutions was to keep chocolate in my car instead of in the house so I would not be tempted to binge but could still have a piece or two if I needed. If this advice isn't something that could be straight out of the Weight Watchers handbook, I don't know what is.

That space was so unsafe that although I was beginning to come to terms with my queerness, I never disclosed it. This experience triggered a relapse back into my eating disorder and a suffocating belief that I was alone in my struggle.

The next time I sought treatment years later, I worked with a dietitian who introduced me to the idea that eating disorders are social justice issues and it was this revelation that completely changed the trajectory of my recovery. In our sessions, I began to learn about how diet culture, fatphobia, and other systems of oppression like racism, ableism, sexism, homophobia, and transphobia are inextricably linked to eating disorders. This knowledge enabled me to start understanding my own experiences within the broader context of a society obsessed with controlling how people's bodies look and act.

Perhaps for me more than most, this was the missing piece to my recovery. As someone who studied social science and is passionate about fighting social injustice, being able to make these connections allowed me to shift my perspective on my own eating disorder experience. While this didn't magically fix my eating disorder, it was critical in alleviating some of the crushing isolation I felt in my recovery. It helped me to better understand that my struggles with food and my body were not just personal issues, but they were also tied up in complex social phenomena.

In many ways, my body holds great privilege. I am white, able-bodied and have never existed in a body too large to fit into aeroplane chairs or mass-produced clothes. However, I do exist in a queer body, I have been brought up in a culture filled with diet culture and interpersonal fatphobia, and I have experienced an eating disorder and recovery in a body which never looked 'thin enough' to meet society's stereotypes of this illness.

This new understanding of how and why my eating disorder operated meant I could heal my experiences of fatphobia and accept my queerness. I am not going to lie: challenging weight discrimination and body standards in a fatphobic world is incredibly tough. Throughout treatment and even more so while in recovery, I have had to learn to manage the dichotomy of trying like hell every day to not engage in eating disorder behaviours while existing in a society which praises dieting, exercise, and controlling one's appearance.

While at first it seemed almost cruel that other people were allowed to intentionally lose weight and be praised for it while for me this behaviour would be seen as a relapse, I now feel grateful that my disorder opened my eyes to the way society praises weight loss without reservation, no matter the cause or method.

I no longer find it triggering when I hear diet talk in social settings. Instead, I try to challenge the fatphobia which plays out in these spaces. The other day, someone said that they needed to lose weight because their pants were getting tight. I said that it sounded like they just needed to buy some new pants.

Sarah Wirth

When I say things like this, I sometimes notice a double take or even a little annoyance or frustration on the person's face as it's not the reaction they expected. I just hope that in these moments, getting a response that doesn't encourage weight loss might, if only for a moment, help someone pause before launching into their newest diet.

With respect to my queerness, I am able to have compassion for myself when I feel uncomfortable in my appearance and instead start questioning society's gendered body ideals for cisgender, transgender, and gender diverse people. In our media, the vast majority of nonbinary representation is people who exist in thin bodies, where the gendered parts of their bodies are minimised and they are able to achieve androgyny with some ease.

What this means is that for many people like me, who still have undeniably gendered body parts like boobs and hips and thighs, being read as anything other than female by society can seem impossible. One of the ways I have tried to feel more comfortable in my body has been through clothing, although this is not a simple solution. There's only so much a binder can do against big boobs and finding men's pants that fit my hips and thighs is no mean feat. While I am acutely aware that losing weight would likely make me feel more comfortable in my gender identity, I also know that this is not and cannot be the solution. Instead, I try and show myself compassion for existing in a world where cisnormativity is the default and remind myself that it is not my body that needs to change but society.

Today, I am proud to be strong in my recovery. These experiences have left me with a passion for helping others to understand how their bodies are shaped by our society and to empower them to challenge body-based oppression and fight for body liberation.

I know that understanding our bodies through a social justice lens might hold the key for many people struggling in eating disorder recovery. I know that this approach can help those in treatment to further understand how their eating disorder developed. I know it can support people to recover back into a society which, at least for now, remains obsessed with body appearance and control.

I know that understanding the connection between social justice and eating disorders is a key to recovery, because it was for me.

How I Learned to Ask for Help in the Forests

Nancy Rechtman

Nancy Rechtman

In January 2020, a dear friend and I booked a bucket-list trip to Costa Rica. We were set to travel in April 2020. You know what happened next. Then we were told that despite having bought travel insurance, our money would not be refunded. Instead, it would be held in a top-secret undisclosed location for safekeeping until such time as the world reopened. Well, not verbatim, but you get the idea. Finally, two-and-a-half years later, the stars realigned, and we were able to head out for the adventure of a lifetime.

Since life is basically a game of Whac-A-Mole, it shouldn't have been a big surprise that obstacles popped up as we eagerly awaited the day we could take this dream trip. The first was an internal leg issue, which makes it difficult for me to put weight on my left leg if I try to do anything other than walk on a flat surface. The second happened last year when I fell and hit my head on the ground with bone-rattling force, ending up in hospital with a brain bleed. This affected my memory, my equilibrium, and pretty much every aspect of my life. I've worked ceaselessly to get back to where I need to be. While I'm not back 100%, I'm much better than I was a year ago, making it possible for me to go on this long-awaited adventure.

Nancy Rechtman

Since day one was a travel day, starting with day two, every day was filled with nonstop action. Activities included hikes through the cloud forest, hikes through the rainforest, walking across hanging bridges, hiking to a volcano, and river rafting. It was like being in a land filled with magic.

I was relieved to discover I was able to meet most challenges unaided. The relief came not only from realising how much I had healed since last year, but also because I wasn't forced to admit my weakness to anyone and ask for help. I will do everything possible to not admit that I can't do everything myself. I had to cave last year when I had the brain injury and accept help when I landed in hospital, and then needed to stay with friends for a few days to recover until I was up to managing on my own.

There was a sky gondola ride that took us to the cloud forest, where we could then hike. A guide accompanied us on the gondola and offered to join us on the hike through the cloud forest. We readily said yes and off we went. We had spectacular views of the lush landscape, and I managed to navigate the trail without issue – until suddenly, there was an issue. We got to a point where the terrain became rocky and uneven, and I was sure I'd go tumbling headfirst down the rocks like an errant matzo ball. So I hesitated. I explained to the guide why I might have to turn back. Yes, that's how meshuga I am. I'd rather turn around than admit I need help.

The very kind young man told me I could hold onto his arm when I felt unsteady, and I could put my foot up against his foot when things got slippery. He said it so matter-of-factly, like of course that's what we should do, that I kept going. I held his arm when necessary, put my foot up against his when I felt like I might start sliding down the inclines, and I made it!

Nancy Rechtman

The second epiphany came when we were walking down a trail to the river where we would get on rafts for a tour through the forest. We had been told to wear our sandals, not our hiking shoes. It was also very rocky and muddy, but again, I managed to make my way down the trail until we came to a steep embankment just before getting to the river. I tried walking sideways. I tried walking slowly. I tried everything I could think of to make my way down that embankment without hurtling over the edge. Frustration and humiliation rose inside me until I stopped in my tracks.

There was one family behind us and I announced that I couldn't move without assistance, and they should go ahead because I didn't want to hold them up. The Jewish martyr syndrome runs strong in my blood. The dad immediately told me to hold on, that he was coming to help me, but before he could move, his daughter and son raced over and each grabbed an arm. They said that they'd get me down. I was so touched that they wanted to help without a moment's hesitation. So we three slowly made our way down the embankment, with me bargaining silently with G-d that if I didn't end up sliding down the incline in slow motion like an arthritic mountain goat, and I didn't pull anyone down with me, I promised to stay off Amazon for a month.

Lo and behold, we made it! Once we reached the water's edge, I did my usual self-deprecating schtick of joking about the experience at my own expense and had everyone laughing as we got into the raft. I was so grateful that the kindness I received allowed me to experience the sights and sounds of the howler monkeys, caimans, sloths, and tropical birds filling the enchanted forest.

Nancy Rechtman

Later, I reflected on these two experiences and I realised that there had been a subtle but definitive shift in my perspective. As I've gotten older, I've become more resistant to asking for help. Over the years, life has taught me that I am essentially on my own.

Then came the brain injury. My friends were there for me without me even asking, like a gaggle of Jewish mothers, fingers wagging in my face if I even tried to refuse their help. As I fought my way back to health, I felt myself making progress, and they all kvelled about each new step in my healing process like I was a baby learning how to walk.

The two events in Costa Rica have indelibly reshaped my way of thinking. I will now occasionally deign to concede that my body is ageing and has suffered injuries that have changed the playing field. I have even accepted the fact that no matter how much I exercise and how healthy I try to eat, I will never have my 25-year-old body back.

In the end, I'm proud of my body. After all that has happened, it still serves me well. I might not be able to do everything unaided, but I can still do a lot. I asked for help – finally – and got to have the time of my life. I know it won't be easy to stop waving people away when they ask if I need assistance, but I celebrate that I'm now receptive to the word 'help.' It has opened up the world for me.

Dog

Meredith Wadley

Meredith Wadley

As a kid, I never had any complaints about my body. It ran when I wanted to run, swam when I leaped into water, pedalled a bike, and jumped horses over fences – even bareback. It slept without much trouble, metabolised the food I ate, and blended in at school, church, the swimming pool, camp, and sleepovers. Really, my body gave me few complaints. Sure, the nails on my fingers and toes grew; I clipped them. And the hair on my head grew; Mom trimmed it. When hair began to grow on my legs and underarms, I learned, not without spilling blood, to shave. My periods came, which wasn't fun, granted, but they were regular and my flow remained minimal – one regular tampon every two hours at its peak. I rarely suffered cramps, and once I became sexually active, I welcomed any spotty arrivals.

While watching TV one evening at the family home, my sister stretched out her legs and said, 'Are my legs pretty?'

'Your legs are very pretty, darling,' Dad said.

She smiled and admired them.

I unfolded my legs. 'Are *mine* pretty?'

Dad grinned. 'Yours are *curvaceous*.'

Quite. They still are, bless them.

My sister's curves developed on her chest. Far more intelligent than me or my brother, she complained about their bounteousness being more desirable than her mind with the boys she dated. Athletic and competitive, she complained about their heaviness. How they created drag when she swam. How they bounced painfully when she rode horses. I did not envy my sister her drag, bounce, or pain. Meanwhile, I remained flat-chested until my first pregnancy, which never bothered me in the least. It came as a shock when I learned that my mom considered my breasts 'underdeveloped.'

'Lucky me,' I thought.

My body and my face never called attention to themselves. Out in the greater world, I enjoyed nothing more than anonymity. Blending in. As I came of age, I watched girlfriends draw attraction and comments from men. Some tried hiding from the attention they garnered. Others acted drawn to it. I remained happy to be in the shadows of what felt instinctively menacing to me. Something predatory or treacherous: the wolf in granny's bed ready to pounce or the shining light luring fragile moth-like girls to self-destruction.

I gave little thought to how my body might appear to others. Of course, as I came of age, I found it awakening to sexual attractions. I blushed over popular boys, allowing one to put his hand down my shirt at the back of the school bus. And I was caught doing so by my sister.

'Why would you *let* someone do that?' she hissed at me later. Two years older than me, she was already burdened by those heavy breasts and her dismay in them; mine had just passed the popped-nipple phase, forming two pleasingly round and smooth mounds. Touch felt lovely.

Meredith Wadley

I told my sister, 'I did it because it *felt* good.' Her mouth fell open in astonishment.

Of course, the magazines we girls pored over were out to sell us bodily dissatisfaction. Without knowing anything about us or our lives, they encouraged us to slim down, dress as if we lived a city girl, artisan, or beach girl's life, change our hairstyles often, and cover our faces with make-up. I wasn't immune to dissatisfaction or self-criticism. I criticised others, too, as one did, and envied the girls in the magazines with their big, wide-set eyes, their teeth as pretty as delicate shells, their limbs long and lean.

However, just one outfit they modelled probably cost more than my budget for a year. The make-up on their faces had been applied by professional hands. And their bodies, as slender as adolescent boys? No amount of dieting would ever transform my curvaceous legs into those of a gazelle. I never found the contents of those magazines inspiring. They simply seemed desperately misinformed and repetitive. I lost interest in their silly content.

Up until I entered middle school, my mom, an expert seamstress, sewed most of the dresses my sister and I wore. Actually, I spent most of my childhood wearing my sister's hand-me-downs. One summer, she shot up in a burst of growth that I never replicated. In contrast to her, I remained a slow and steady grower, and at some point, teenager me owned a closetful of four-year-old fashions designed for pre-adolescent tastes. I did have my limits, though, and begged for new store-bought clothes.

Mom and I drove to the local mall where we split up, agreeing to meet at a specified time in a specified place. When the time approached, I headed to the agreed-upon place just past the mall's central feature, an indoor fountain. A glass cupola flooded the sparkling water with light, and its steady spray drowned out the conversations of people milling about. Kids in strollers held colourful balloons. An elderly couple licked ice cream cones, and between shoppers with bags at their feet, a group of boys my age sat on the circular wall of the fountain pool. The boys seemed to be looking for someone, and I briefly caught the eye of one. His companions noticed and nudged him. Smiling sheepishly, he stood. I looked behind me to see the object of his attention, noticing only a crowd of bodies on the move. Short and tall. Light and dark. Young and old. Paired, with children, or alone. Long haired. Short haired. Bald. None stood out. I turned back, and the boy from the fountain stood in front me, blocking my way. I stepped aside. He followed, his eyes sparking. Something seemed off. I stopped, and he glanced at his friends. They nodded and grinned uniformly as if to say, 'Go on! Do it!'

He did.

'Dog!' he shouted.

My jaw dropped as he spun on his heels and rushed to rejoin his friends. The row of them grabbed their sides and buckled, howling with laughter. Like baseball players, they slapped my antagonist on his back as he settled among them, another sheepish grin marking his face like a fresh scar.

A voice in my head said, 'So, there it is, Meredith. You're a dog.' If I'd never thought about how I appeared to others – especially anyone I longed to attract – I now knew. 'That's how the world sees you. A *dog*, Meredith,' the voice said. 'A dog.' The voice, of course, was my own. And I neither questioned it nor the boy from the fountain.

On the drive home, I played the scene over and over.

'Cat got your tongue?' my mom said.

I shrugged.

'Something wrong?'

Not *wrong*, really. Not wrong, knowing how others saw me. *Informing,* more like. Hurtful, too, but—

We left the Sunset Highway and climbed the rolling hills to our house, cocooned in a forest of Douglas firs.

Freeing, I decided.

If boys saw me as a 'dog,' then why not go with it? I didn't have to waste time or money making myself attractive or learning to flirt. I could simply be myself, as I'd always been, unencumbered by worrying over other people's judgements and expectations.

A fresh and vibrant spring landscape sped by. It was tempting to stick my head out the window.

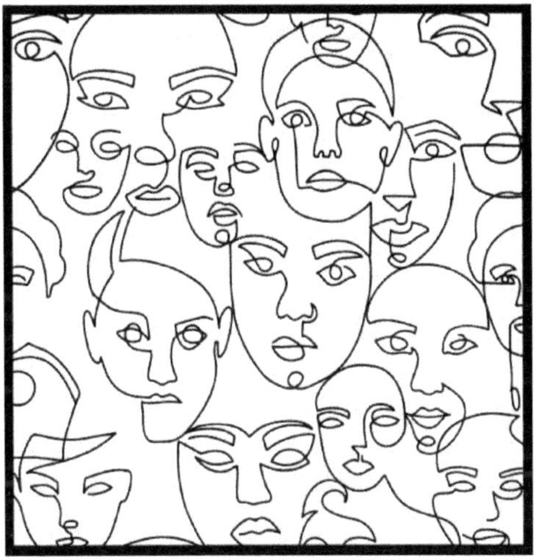

Afterword

When projects start to take shape, there can be a chorus of 'Well, we weren't expecting *that*!' from their creators. Stories became increasingly interconnected and with each new book in this series, we found ourselves more and more entangled. The first anthology, packed with essays about the ins and outs (ha!) of sex, seemed straight-forward at the time. We asked writers to share their personal experiences about the good, bad, and embarrassing, and they did, in many wonderful ways.

Then came the second book. This one was about parenthood, and once again we received umpteen brilliantly told tales about all the sides of parenting, whether being (or not being) parented or being (and not being) a parent. And we started to worry a little that our topics were blending into each other. We didn't think about the relationship between sex and parenting (well, obviously aside from *that* part), and how parenthood wreaks havoc on sex and sexuality, or how our feelings about sex impact our decisions – or lack of – around parenting.

When the time came to choose the theme for the third anthology, we realised we had dug ourselves a neat little hole. Our relationships with our bodies cannot be described without connecting them to parenthood, or to sex. Stories about how parenting has ruined bodies, or damaged parent-child relationships; stories about how bodies are intricately linked to sex, even unintentionally: the essays we consume in these three anthologies are all interwoven in visible and invisible ways. We examine our relationships between our body, our family, our sexuality. We, as readers, can identify parts of ourselves in the experiences of others. We can look critically at these parts under a spotlight, turning them over, learning how these small pieces of ourselves come together to make us the uniquely proud, neurotic, embarrassed, joyful humans that we are.

While this was wholly unexpected, it ended up being quite beautiful too, because isn't the wall that keeps us from becoming who we were meant to be made up of many bricks? If we were a bit better organised, you'd think we planned it (we aren't, and we didn't.) Once again we are grateful and honoured to showcase the amazing authors whose deeply personal, sometimes funny, sometimes enraging stories appear in this book. We are in awe of both your courage and your talent, and so pleased you chose us to share your stories. Thank you all for trusting us.

We tried something new with this book: crowdfunding. We asked for your help to produce the third *Keeping It Under Wraps* anthology, and you came through. To those who supported us through donations, who cheered us on, who listened to us rant or marvel, depending on the day, to the ones who showed up when we needed you: a thousand thanks.

A special thanks to our Kickstarter supporters

Riv Begun

Shereena-Lee van de Berkt

Sarah Buchmann

Marina Cellitti

Yao Chang

Nicole Cunningham

Lorraine Curran-Vu

Kaitlin Felix

Stephen "Chucky" Hope

Andrea Hurley

Karen Irby

Lady Jessica

Christine Knudsen

Kristina

Kaitlynn Leal

Inze van der Lei

Alex Liu

M

Emma McKay

Daryl Miller

Katie Moore

Barbara Nigg

Helle Norup

Protocolocon

Asma Rehan

Lisa Romeo

Jen Rye

Rachel Strange

C.S. Wilde

Erin W.

We couldn't have published this anthology without your help.
Thank you all for your support and trust.

Have you read the first two Keeping Under Wraps books?

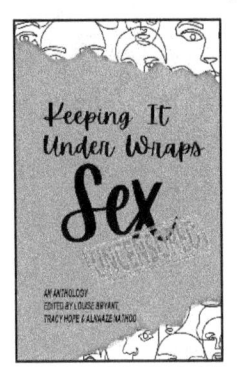

A Recommended Read by **BookMuse**
Featured on **CapeTalk Radio** with **Sara-Jayne King.**

Such a unique and individual anthology which challenges people's perceptions of sex and works towards ending the stigma around discussing this 'taboo' topic.
- **Bex Books and Stuff** -

The range of perspectives is wonderful with plenty of opportunities to consider the wide range of human experience with sex - from nodding in agreement to involuntary eyebrow raising.
- **Goodreads** -

No matter your literary tastes, you will find a story in this book that will hit close to home, and you will know then, that you're not alone. An absolute must read.
- **Author C.S. Wilde** -

I found this book a refreshing read - unlike anything I have read before!
- **Momo Book Diary** –

...this book is an absolute triumph. An outstanding collection of the highest merit and quality, and a composition worthy of the utmost respect for every single contributor... From a literary point of view, it is tremendous. From a social commentary point of view, it is essential.
- Author Matt McAvoy –

All of these stories are deeply personal, honest and evocative. Reading this book was a privilege, the honesty of the authors something to be respected and not taken lightly.
- Bex Books and Stuff –

You realize you may be alone in the dark with a screeching toddler or struggling with infertility or being the child of inadequate parents and you will have a hand in the dark squeezing yours and you'll know you're not the only one who's felt that way.
- Amazon review -

Discover the many stories shared in our previous anthologies; pick up the *Keeping Up It Under Wraps* books today.
Available in print and electronic formats worldwide online and from all good bookshops.

Sign up for the latest news from

Keeping It Under Wraps

Get updates from the KIUW editorial team, including industry tips and submission opportunities for writers and new stories from KIUW authors.

SCAN ME

Or visit keepingitunderwraps.com.

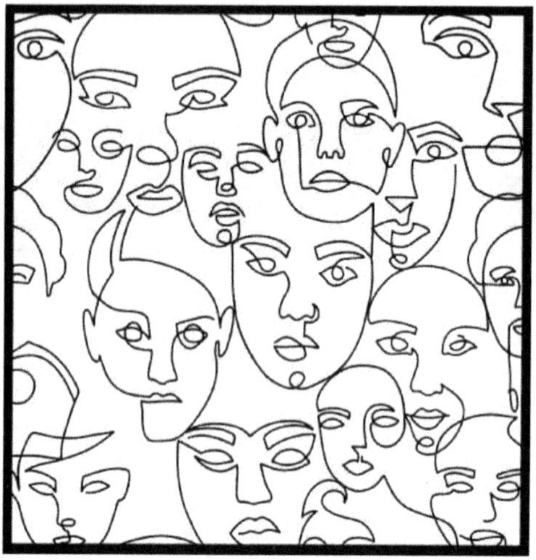